SERENITY IN MOTION

INNER PEACE: ANYTIME, ANYWHERE

NANCY O'HARA

WARNER BOOKS

An AOL Time Warner Company

Copyright © 2003 by Nancy O'Hara
All rights reserved.

Warner Books, Inc., 1271 Avenue of the Americas, New York, NY 10020
Visit our Web site at www.twbookmark.com.

 An AOL Time Warner Company

Printed in the United States of America
First Printing: November 2003
10 9 8 7 6 5 4 3 2 1

Library of Congress Cataloging-in-Publication Data

O'Hara, Nancy.
    Serenity in motion : inner peace—anytime, anywhere / Nancy O'Hara.
      p. cm.
      ISBN 0-446-69085-6
      1. Peace of mind. I. Title
BF637.P3O42 2003
158.1—dc21   2003043263

Book design and text composition by L&G McRee
Cover design by Brigid Pearson

To Michael

with all my heart
thank you for being so brave
and teaching me that which I most need to learn

Contents

Introduction xi
    Belly-Mind xvi

1. *The Practice of Being Still* 1
    Listening 5
    Standing 7
    Sitting 10
    Waiting 12
    Watching TV 14
    Being Patient 16

2. *The Practice of Being in Motion* 19
    Walking 21
    Talking 24
    Eating 26
    Playing 28
    Tasking 30
    Driving 33

BATHING 36
WORKING 38

3. *The Practice of Being Challenged* 41
EGO..43
RELATIONSHIPS..45
FAILURE...47
SUCCESS...49
FRUSTRATION 51
DISAPPOINTMENT 53
AMBITION 55
OPPORTUNITY 58
COMPETING AND COMPARING 60
LOVE 63

4. *The Practice of Being Present* 67
BROKEN SHOELACES...69
CHOCOLATE 71
THE WEATHER 73
CHANGE...74
MONEY...77
SEX...78

5. *The Practice of Letting Go* 83
    DEATH 85
    ILLNESS 88
    LOSS 90
    BIRTH 92
    CELEBRATIONS 94
    VACATIONS 96
    JOB LOSS 98

6. *The Practice of Being Aware* 103
    PAIN 105
    NEGATIVITY 108
    HOPE 110
    JEALOUSY 113
    MOODS 114
    FEAR 116
    JOY 119
    ANGER 120

Closing Thoughts 123
    CURIOSITY 123
    ABOUT THE AUTHOR 126

Introduction

My first book, *Find a Quiet Corner*, is an introduction to the practice of mindful breathing. It stresses the importance of setting aside time in your day to concentrate on this practice so that you can gain some peace of mind. There are many suggestions in it of how to find the time, where to set up your quiet corner, and what to do once you're there. If you haven't yet read it, you might want to take a look at it, but you needn't have read it to gain something from this book. (And you can wait to read it or choose not to read it at all, though it will add to your understanding if you do.) *Serenity in Motion* builds on the practices developed in *Find a Quiet Corner* and brings them into the rest of your life.

The remedy for all your woes is very simple, but as you may know by now it truly is not easy to put into practice. Some of you may have established a quiet corner at home to which you retreat at the beginning or end of your day in order to draw on your spiritual energy for guidance or to replenish the energy you've spent that day. Some of you, who regularly find the time to spend in your quiet corner, have reaped the rewards of this experience and live in harmony with the changing circumstances of your life. And some of you no longer resist what happens in your life and have come to welcome the unexpected. Yet you may find that spending time each day sitting quietly alone, focused on your breath, letting your thoughts float by without getting attached to them, doesn't always guarantee serenity. It can be threatened at any moment and in certain situations throughout the day. Sometimes, even before we are aware of it, we get caught in a whirlwind of actions or feelings that carries us into a storm of confusion. Our day gets upset, we blame ourselves or others, we project into the future, and we sit in disharmony until we can get back to our quiet corner and set ourselves back on course.

The good news is that you needn't wait to return to your quiet corner to reestablish your equanimity. You can carry the practices from your quiet corner into all of life's circumstances and employ them at any time. Thus, each day can be a rich and gratifying experience, where everything that happens is not only okay, but is exactly as it should be.

Just as it takes practice to hone the skills you learn in your quiet corner, so will it take practice to carry them with you and use them on all and sundry occasions as you face the daily vicissitudes of your life.

The complexity of our lives, the daily challenges that we encounter, and the myriad large and small decisions that we continually must make, can challenge even the most serene of us. Yet even as we resist it, most of us are up to this challenge—because we intuitively know that we can rise above it all and disallow it to defeat us.

So let this book be your guide until you can tap into your own intuitive reservoir for all the solutions. Here you will find suggestions for dealing with some typical issues that might come your way on any given day. Keep in mind that it cannot cover every possible scenario. Your life is unique, as are your particular life's circumstances, not to mention the feelings and personality that you bring to everything. No one can know without a doubt what the future holds. In the end it is up to you to meet each moment as it arrives—with honesty, integrity, and an open and willing heart.

All it takes is a decision. Not just one decision, but many throughout each day. Make a vow to yourself at the start of your day and renew it as often as necessary as the day progresses. This is the key to serenity. This is about accepting that each new moment is just that—new. And that no one moment can be duplicated exactly. This will give you a fresh start, a new opportunity to reinvent yourself every moment and live fully and completely, aware and awake, present in the magnanimous now.

Serenity in Motion is a primer for learning how to approach the world without reservation, fear, or self-imposed impediments. It is a tool to use while you train yourself to rely on yourself. Carry it with you, refer to it, and take the suggestions. Try new ways of looking at situations, of communicating with others, of seeing the world. Then start to take bigger risks and, finally, let your intuition guide you. Trust it. It will never fail you or let you down. And if you maintain a positive attitude, your worries will not overwhelm you. And most of all: remember to laugh. Simply laugh and be grateful for your life. In the end it is all you have.

There are a few main themes or threads running through *Serenity in Motion*. They are:

- Embrace whatever it is that pains you
- Loosen the tight hold you have on people, places, and things; good and bad
- Just breathe
- Expect nothing
- Keep a positive attitude

- Cultivate a sense of gratitude
- Pay attention and
- Practice, practice, practice

Some of these may seem contradictory, like embracing something only to then let go. Think of it instead as a paradox that's not supposed to make conceptual sense. Right here, right now, is the perfect opportunity to practice these two suggestions. Here's how: embrace your confusion; don't let it detain you or stop you from moving on. Allow yourself to be confused and then keep going. Once you've accepted your confusion, fully and completely, you no longer have a need to hold on. Just let go. Relax your grasp on it. And then notice how easy it is to let go once you've embraced it, compared to how impossible it was to resist it, push it away, and make it disappear.

Anytime you get stuck, refer to this simple exercise and practice it on the spot. Keep practicing it until it becomes second nature. Strive for perfection but don't expect it. You may never reach perfection, but you will come to understand that the process itself is perfect.

BELLY-MIND

One other important concept woven throughout the text is that of *belly-mind*, often referred to as *hara*, which literally translates as belly or "gut." Many spiritual teachers throughout history have taught this concept in a variety of ways. Belly-mind is a "place" deep within us that guides us in spiritual matters. It is a place that defies logic and holds our answers. Some say it is the seat of intuition. In the Zen tradition *hara* is said to be our center of gravity, located about two inches below our navel. It is the center that holds your inner truth, the center that is home for your spirit, the center from which serenity arises.

Nothing can be done without using the muscles in our abdomen. When we cry, laugh, fight, or make love we use these muscles. Whenever we move a body part or exert energy of any sort we must necessarily use our abdominal muscles. The principal of belly-mind purports that when we create tension in our bellies, and concentrate our energy there, we create physical and mental stability. Breathing deeply into our bellies can also control our thoughts and habitual reactions. The breath draws attention to the hara and away from ego-driven thought. This focused mindfulness generates all the spiritual power you will need to be in a continual state of alert and wakeful serenity, where nothing is "wrong" and everything makes "sense."

At all times, whether sitting still or moving around, concentrate on this place in your body. Breathe from there, think from there, move from there. Retrain your first brain into thinking of this gut feeling or "second brain" as its master. Imagine that you are carrying around a red-hot ball of fire located in your belly just below your navel. When your attention strays from there and rises up, immediately drop it back down to this center of gravity by using your breath as the transport. Think of it as a life-and-death matter—you must operate from this place no matter what.

Although it is not easy to be concentrated on your belly every second while sitting still, it is even more challenging to do it while moving around. Right now as you read these words draw them into your belly. Focus completely on your belly until you are just one big belly brain, breathing and laughing through to the end of this page and then on to the rest of your day.

Don't settle for less than total belly absorption. Commit yourself to this practice. Make a vow to yourself right now that you will carry belly-mind into everything that you do, think, feel, see, hear, say, smell, and breathe. Trust the spiritual teachers who have come before us and identified this belly-mind as your spiritual center; trust also that all your troubles are spiritual maladies that have spiritual solutions. If you are dedicated, and if you carry this mindful practice with you twenty-four hours a day, there is no question that you will have a contented, meaningful life. Trust that. And if you don't trust yet, allow yourself to doubt, and breathe that into your belly. Breathe in the doubt and breathe out trust. If you truly want meaning and serenity in your life, live from your belly.

The Practice of Being Still

We can be moving at a furious pace even when we're not in motion. This activity is usually our mind working overtime, which can cause stress, distress, anxiety, and health problems. The solution then is simple: slow down the movement of our mind.

But when our mind continues to move, even after our body is quiet, it can keep us from making the effort to be still, which moves us even further away from a calm mind. Our mind keeps chattering once we've stilled our body because our mind doesn't want us to be still. When we are still, our mind inevitably slows down and is no longer in charge. But our mind, and most especially our petty-ego, wants to be in charge; it is not happy when it's not, so it does everything in its power to keep us moving. And it usually wins.

So then the question becomes: how do we take charge of our mind? You might also wonder: isn't my mind me? If I'm not in charge of my own mind, then who or what is? Good questions. Put them aside for a moment and consider this: if you were truly in charge of your mind, wouldn't you just be able to say to it: calm down, relax, don't worry, stop thinking so much, and other similar things? Haven't we all tried such coaxing? Has it ever worked?

So now what? Well, the good news is that there is a way to take charge. Rather than fighting fire with fire, pitting will against will, you can learn another approach to relieve the pressure, quiet your mind, and let go of the need for answers.

What is this miraculous way? What do we use, if not our will, to calm ourselves and become masters of our minds?

Breath.

It's really quite simple. Almost too simple for our complicated minds to understand and accept.

Breath.

It may seem like there must be more to it, but the answer is: not really.

It is simply a matter of concentrating and bringing your

attention to your breath. The key concept here is concentration. This is where your indomitable will can be utilized. Draw all of your energy and spirit into each breath; and as you do, draw your breath deeper and deeper into your belly-mind. Each time your mind strays, gently draw it back as you would a windblown scarf, and concentrate with all your might and attention on each inhalation and each exhalation. This is not an easy task. Each time, thoughts and sounds and disappointments will disturb you. But there will come a point when you will experience, for a fraction of a second, such full concentration on your breathing that all thoughts and outside interference will halt. This "space between thoughts" is where your truth resides, where your essence is revealed. Eventually, with practice, these moments will get longer, and you will completely lose yourself in the practice of concentrated breathing, deep in your belly. Then you will know why this practice is so valuable. You will experience contentment as never before; and a deep understanding will prevail. But even before this, when you engage in this concentrated breath practice each day, for fifteen, twenty, forty minutes, a number of things happen:

- your body slows down
- your breath gets deeper

- your mind follows and begins to slow down (sometimes kicking and screaming, but eventually giving in peacefully)
- your heart rate slows
- anger, depression, and anxiety abate
- pain symptoms relax
- plus much more

You have the power to manifest these benefits. So concentrate, keep a positive attitude, and breathe your way to serenity.

As you become more aware of your breath, you will naturally cultivate a spirit of gratitude for your breath—because it equals life. Prior to this breath-attention practice you most likely took your breath for granted. But no longer. Once you stop taking your life-source for granted you will extend this same attitude to all other things and people and circumstances. You might have to remind yourself now and then, but if you keep up the breath-awareness practice then the practice of gratitude will automatically follow.

LISTENING

How many of us know how to really listen? Do we know how to listen to our own mind as it careens out of control and races off on some tangent or other, into the past or the future? Or to others—our co-workers, loved ones, or strangers—as they attempt to communicate something to us? To the everyday sights, sounds, and sensations that surround us? Even if we think of ourselves as good listeners, and are seen that way by others, it is wise to be open to the idea that there is always more to learn, that there are deeper levels of hearing we can access.

The practice of listening can be done anywhere at any time. Opportunities to hone your listening skills are presented to you throughout each day. All that is required is to still yourself and pay attention. Once you decide to really listen, bring your whole body into the activity, not just your ears and your brain. You do this naturally anyway, but I invite you to witness yourself doing it and then expand upon this power. The very next time you hear a pleasant sound—a child's laughter or a church bell—stop and pay attention; breathe it into you. Listen to it with your gut, your belly, your toes. Do it right now as you read this. Listen to the room sounds in this way. Same thing with an unpleasant sound—police sirens or traffic noise. First notice your reaction and resistance to it, your impulse to will it away, and how that affects your body. Then invite the sound in (what other choice do you have?) and notice the difference. Rather than let any sound, pleasant or unpleasant, become a distraction, allow it to be part of your environment, part of your personal space. Be with the sounds, move with them, and give up the battle to control them.

Here's an exercise that can be practiced every time you exchange words with someone else:

First, as they speak to you, notice your reaction to them. Are you thinking about how their message affects you, how to respond to them, or what they need from you? Do you find yourself interjecting comments or gestures to signal to them that you're listening? How much of your listening is about you rather than about them?

Second, experiment with the notion that it's okay for you to say nothing. Then just listen and curb your desire to jump in, to insert yourself. Wait until they've said all they want to say before you speak. If there's silence, as they struggle to formulate an idea or reach for some word, let the silence be okay. Don't rush to fill it. Practice being silent and just listening.

Engage a friend in this listening exercise: take turns speaking and listening. Choose a topic to talk about—your boss, your partner, a recent experience, or a career ambition—and then spend five minutes listening, as your friend speaks, and five minutes speaking, as your friend listens. When you listen, just listen—in stillness and in silence. In no time you will see that when you free yourself of the obligation to respond, not only do you become a better listener, but also your partner feels heard in a new and expansive way.

STANDING

Standing still is anathema to so many these days. Our lives are about movement, about doing, about getting someplace. We so rarely are where we are. Instead, we're into the next thing, place, thought, or action before we even get there. And then when we do get there we hardly take the time to be there, as we're off into the next whatever. We are racing to catch up with ourselves, which usually leaves us stressed out and short of breath, hoping everything will stop, and wondering whence relief will come. We even chase after relief, even though it is eternally out of reach when we do chase it.

If this is all true, it seems that the solution is to just stop. But because this is nearly impossible to contemplate, let alone accomplish, we feel defeated before we even begin. We've tried slowing down before with little success. The surprise here is that you are already doing what you need to do and the only thing now is to take advantage of those already existing moments.

Standing. At the bus stop, the copier, or ATM machine. In the theater or grocery store checkout line. Waiting for the elevator to arrive or the stoplight to change. Throughout the day we frequently find ourselves standing with no place to go, and too often we squander this time. Anxious for movement, we view the stillness, the lack of motion, as a waste of time. Paradoxically, when we're on life's treadmill all we want to do is stop. Yet when we do we yearn to move. Just one example of never being satisfied with where we are.

All it takes to transform these moments from dreadful to delicious is a little mind movement, a shift in attitude. Even if you cannot go directly to a new outlook, if you're reading this you most likely have the willingness to take a different approach. And if you're willing, then change is possible.

When your body comes to a standstill your mind doesn't

always follow right away, which is why not moving can create such internal discomfort. So when you find yourself standing still with your mind on fast forward, there are two things you can do.

One, become aware of your body in space, where it is, how it feels. Notice your posture and any tension you might have in your spine. Make slight adjustments to how you're standing and breathe into your whole back as you center your awareness on the fact that you are able to stand upright. Feel your feet standing firmly on the ground. Imagine that there are roots solidly planting you into the earth, your legs the trunk of a tree, your upper body the branches gently swaying in the breeze. If you're carrying heavy bags, place them down as you stand there, unburdened and free. Appreciate your body; savor the moment. Be there with every inch of every fiber of your being.

Two, once you've stilled your body, observe your mind and where it wants to take you physically, mentally, and emotionally. Watch your thoughts; simply stand there, breathe into your belly, be in your body, and pay attention—without judgment or criticism. Consider that everyone around you, standing with you, contains a similarly active mind. It might take time, but know that if you still your body the mind will eventually follow and reach a state of stillness—the first step to serenity.

And keep in mind that there are no needless, wasted moments. Each one is precious and an opportunity to experience contentment. So stand tall in your life with all that it offers, good and bad, and know that serenity is available in and through everything. Be sure to stand wherever you are and you won't miss it.

SITTING

Although we may find ourselves sitting down through much of the day, how many of us ever make a conscious decision to just sit? Usually when we're sitting, we are also driving or eating or working or watching a movie or relaxing. Sitting is usually about something other than just sitting. And if we've ever contemplated the idea of sitting for the sake of sitting, perhaps we've concluded that it would be a simple waste of time—so even if we've been advised to do it, we often choose not to. Just the thought of sitting and doing nothing may terrify us, especially when it's linked to the word "meditation." Take this moment and discard all your preconceived notions of what sitting still is all about. Drop the word "meditation" from your vocabulary. And then allow yourself to be open to sitting in a new way.

Just sitting. Here you will find the source for your serenity. Just sitting. Here you will develop a practice of being still that you can then bring into all your other activities. Just sitting. This is the only suggestion in this book that it's best not to skip.

So take a seat with the clear intention to just sit. Begin with five or ten minutes and use your body and your breath to do it. Let your mind come along for the ride, or in this case "the sit." Concentrate on your posture (erect), your breathing (deep and slow), and your fingers and toes (relaxed). Begin each session with closed eyes in order to draw your attention inward. Then once you're focused, gently open your eyes and just breathe. Nothing to do. Nowhere to go. Watch as your mind tries to pull you away from any discomfort you might experience. Breathe deeply into your belly. Expect nothing. Simply and gently, just sit and breathe. Practice being still. The longer you still your body, and the deeper into your belly you breathe, the quieter your mind will become. This practice of sitting still and doing nothing will eventually create space between thoughts. This space will hold pure, intrinsic awareness. This will be the breeding ground for serenity—not just as you sit, but at all times. So sit still and discover this internal mechanism for creating peace and harmony within, no matter what is going on outside. Then you can carry it with you always and tap into it whenever you need it.

WAITING

Waiting. We all do it. We wait for the movie to start, the train to come, the weekend, our vacation. We can't wait until we meet the "right" partner, we're in the perfect job, or we have more money. What we're really doing in all these situations is waiting for our life to happen. Waiting for the next thing. Biding our time. It isn't your fault, you might say—"the train isn't here yet" or "I'm so unhappy in my job." Perhaps. But consider this: the train may never come. Then what? Your life will have been about just waiting. If this idea doesn't appeal to you, then you can begin to transform your waiting time into being-present time.

One way to convert the "waiting" into "being" is with language. All it takes is some willingness and then awareness. Each time you notice yourself using the word "wait," change it to something else. For instance, "I'm waiting for the train, it's late again" can be changed to "I'm at the train station. My train isn't on schedule. That gives me time to read undistracted. What a gift." From negative, biding-time language to positive, present-moment language. Feel the difference? And once your language changes, your attitude and behavior will change. And then peace of mind will be close at hand.

Usually we get irritated if we find ourselves waiting for something or someone, because we feel duped. We did not schedule the waiting time into our day, we are in a hurry to get to the next thing, and we feel at the mercy of some outside force. All of which makes us feel like victims. But if we can see the flip side of this and admit that it is not something being done to us, it is just something that happens, we can then react in a more positive way and use it to our advantage.

Waiting can be an opportunity, a gift of time, to spend constructively, frivolously, or however else you choose. Use it to do the crossword puzzle or read that magazine you never have time to otherwise. Daydream or write a love letter that you may never send. Strike up a conversation with a stranger. Not to pass the time, but to be present in time. Notice how time expands when you're waiting for something else to happen. The seconds seem to tick by slower than usual. Rather than defining this as lost time, see it as found time; as time that moves slowly, time that you can be in and savor. Once you rephrase your approach to this waiting period, settle down into it and let the power of it, the gift of it, wash over you and create stillness in your mind. You will see how easy this is to do once you do it the first time. Coax your mind back from its destination—where you expected to be once the "waiting" is over—and be present in your current circumstances. You will learn soon enough that you can't be anywhere else. So why not be here and enjoy it? Otherwise, one day your life will be over and you won't remember how you got there.

WATCHING TV

When you watch television do you do it mindlessly, hoping to relax and put out of your mind the travails of the day? Do you ever sit for hours in front of the tube to escape your usual life? Do you do it for lack of something else to do? Do you always have it on in the background even if you're not sitting and watching it? Do you sometimes feel guilty after watching it, sure that you could have spent the time more productively?

Whatever your answers to these questions may be, the bottom line is that if you have a TV in your house you have a relationship with it. If you don't have a TV, you can substitute your computer, CD player, radio, or telephone here. In any case, your relationship with your appliances can be improved—by employing the tools of mindfulness and concentration. Two tools that we will be using throughout this book to nurture serenity and contentedness.

Mindfulness first. If there's a particular show you're fond of or you want to wind down from your day, make the decision to watch TV and set the time aside exclusively for this purpose. Consciously choosing to turn it on and watch, rather than slipping into an old habitual pattern, is the first step to mindful viewing. Then sit down and just watch the program. Don't eat, read, clean, or do anything else as you watch TV. Mindfully pay attention to what you are watching, to where you are sitting as you watch, to how you're feeling, and what your enjoyment level is.

Then concentrate on just watching your show. No strain or exertion. Simply concentrate on what you've chosen to do. Be there with the TV, just you and it. Even if family members are watching with you this can still be your exercise, with you and the TV. No one else need even know what you're doing.

Spend a week or two mindfully concentrating on this activity of sitting still and just watching. Take notice of the various realizations that arise in connection with this practice. Are you enjoying TV more or less this way? Does it make you want to watch more or less often? What have you discovered about yourself vis-à-vis your habits of television watching?

This practice is not intended to curb or increase the time you spend watching TV. It is meant merely to guide you toward consciously and mindfully choosing when and what to watch so that your serenity is not compromised. Once you know what works best for you, give yourself permission to occasionally indulge in some mindless TV watching, just so long as you mindfully make that choice; give yourself the freedom not to punish yourself or feel guilty. And then, enjoy.

BEING PATIENT

No matter how quickly we want things to change or how much we want things, people, situations to be different than they are or how much we want, period, the wisest choice is usually to do nothing. This is the ultimate being-still practice. Doing nothing seems like just that: nothing. Perhaps on the surface it looks that way, but when we do nothing there is a lot going on. This something is called life.

Consider the word "life" for just a moment. What is it? See if you can detach from what you call your life and become an observer, a detached anthropologist of what it is you call your life. Can you see that you cannot know how events in your life will evolve? Can you see that your life has energy with or without your hands on the controls and that it usually goes much smoother if you let go? Can you feel the calm that results from stepping aside for these few moments as you observe this phenomenon called your life, and let life live you rather than you living life?

If you do not experience these things right away, do not worry. Practicing the patience to let life events unfold on their own will give you an opportunity to truly participate in your life rather than continually trying to control the outcome, the results, the solution. And this practice will lead to equanimity and a life filled with life. Ask yourself, what more could you want? As you continue to practice patience, you will know that all is as it should be and your job is simply to show up and ask each day how you can be of service to yourself, your loved ones, and your life. And remember that all answers will be revealed, as my spiritual teacher is fond of saying, "with the readiness of time."

To put it another way, being patient is simply this: just being and expecting nothing.

The Practice of Being in Motion

There is a grave misconception that serenity can only be had while meditating, and that meditation can only be done in a quiet room with no distractions. Many people think that meditation is a break from life, a mind vacation, a time-out from the usual. And that if we do this, if we take these breaks, then the rest of our life will run smoothly.

While there is some truth to this, mostly it's an unbalanced view of what meditation is and how it can work in our lives. The most important thing to know is that meditation is not a withdrawal from life, it is an extension of it. And while it is crucial to sit still, as described in the previous section, if we limit our opportunities for spiritual growth and serenity to the times when we are still, we will be doing ourselves a disservice, especially since most of our time is spent other than sitting still.

Sitting still is merely the foundation for building a complete life of serenity. We cannot do without it. But just as a foundation alone does not make a home, sitting still by itself does not make a serene life. And just as a house will crumble and fall without a foundation, so will our life if we do not practice sitting still. But there is more to a calm mind than just sitting still. Once we begin our sitting-still practice we can then take what we learn there and apply it everywhere else. The first place we can use it—the place where we are most of the time—is the place of being in motion. And being in motion and approaching it as practice is a lovely way to engage with life and nurture your serenity.

The most vital element of this practice is mindfulness. In the practice of being still you learned about concentration, about paying attention, about listening, about constantly bringing yourself back to your breath, your belly-mind, or to other being-still moments. This is the beginning of mindfulness. So many of us reside either in the past or in the future. We obsess about what did or didn't happen or what will or won't happen next. Our minds become filled with worry or anxiety. Mindfulness is the cure to an overflowing, chattering, busy mind. With mindfulness we simply draw our attention to the present moment, activity, feeling. We pay attention to what is happening right now by concentrating on the action itself. Lose yourself in what you are doing. Get rid of the idea "I am doing" or "I am feeling" and just do, just feel. When you are self-conscious you cannot concentrate on anything. Freedom from self-consciousness through mindfulness allows for a creative and productive moment, day, and life.

When mindfulness is practiced, thoughts of the past or the future begin to recede and you become present to what is happening now. When you are present your life does not pass you by as you wait for it to happen. It happens as you live it. It cannot be any other way. The truth and power of this will be revealed as soon as you begin to practice mindfulness. You can do this anyplace, at any time—being still or being in motion. And from this you can build your own temple of serenity.

WALKING

Buddha said of himself and his monks: "When we walk, we know we are walking." This is a beautiful practice and one of the simplest and most immediately rewarding and instructive. It is both grounding and freeing. The benefits suit our need for immediate gratification because they begin to appear with the first step. And they are endless. All you have to do is be present with each step.

Rather than focus on your destination, gather yourself with each breath and bring your attention to the activity of walking. Set some time aside to spend just walking, or each time you find yourself walking from one place to the next be mindful of what you are doing and put out of your mind where you are going. Bring your awareness to the walking and put aside the idea that it is a means to an end. If you can be there, present, alert, mindful, as you take steps and move your body across the earth and through space, then you will be there for your life. Which is not a race to the end—even if some days it may feel that way. It is just life, and yours at that.

So whether you set time aside to just walk or you take advantage of the various times throughout the day when you're walking, do it mindfully. Begin by counting your steps, one-to-ten, one-to-ten. This will bring your attention into your body, into the act of walking. Then, as you continue to count your steps bring your attention to your breath. Don't alter your step or your breath, just draw all your attention to them. Notice how many steps you take on each inhale, on each exhale. Notice your impulse to stop, to think of where you're going, to move faster. And then just count and breathe. As your rhythm modulates, count the steps you take on each inhalation, and each exhalation. Inhale, one-two-three. Exhale, one-two-three. Just notice, breathe, and count. Start to become aware of the surrounding environment. Be in it, be present, be mindful. It is not about how fast or slow you move, it is only about being present in each step you take. Walk toward having the number of steps you take on the inhalation equal the number of steps you take on the exhalation. And then every so often take an extra step on the exhale; lengthen your exhalation.

If you discover that you move so fast through life that mindful walking is near impossible, because each time you make the effort to slow down your body your mind continues to speed ahead, do not be discouraged. Do not, at first, intentionally slow your physical movement. Keep your normal pace, and within that movement, little by little, start to pay attention to your breath, to each step. You may not be able to sustain mindful attention the whole distance from your house to the car or bus, but if a portion of that walk is taken mindfully it is a good beginning. Each day add one more breath to this mindfulness practice. Be patient and trust that if you walk with your body your mind will eventually follow. Both will reach a calm place if you continue the practice. So just walk and let each moment reveal its unique mystery. Then, each time you walk, you will know that you are walking.

TALKING

Paying attention to the words we use and the effect they have on others, ourselves, and on our own level of serenity is just the beginning of using this everyday activity to deliver tranquillity into each day. Just as we can adopt good and bad habits of behavior, so can we do this with our patterns of speech. At times, we are completely unaware of what we are saying. Paying attention is crucial.

There are two aspects to this talk-practice, one being deconstructive, the other constructive.

Notice when your serenity is disturbed after you have had a conversation with someone. Review what it was that you said and think about how you would change it if you could have the conversation again. Of course, you won't get a second chance, but new opportunities to talk in a different way will continue to arise. Don't get caught in the trap of feeling that the other person's words should be different—you have no control over that. Over time, notice your speech patterns and decide to use your words differently on the next occasion presented to you. Perhaps you will notice that you say too much or too little or that your tone is blaming or hostile. Maybe you will notice that you use self-defeating or self-deprecating language. Whatever it is, do not judge it; simply decide that you'd like to change it.

On the constructive side of this talk-practice, when you're engaged in conversation use positive, upbeat language. Do not lie, gossip, or engage in frivolous conversation. This may seem like a tall order, and you may not even be aware that you do it. Every one of us is probably guilty of it at times. While it may seem like innocent fun, keep in mind that words are very powerful and it is your responsibility to use language wisely. It isn't necessary to be self-righteous when others attempt to seduce you into gossip. Simply change the subject or communicate that you'd rather not participate in the conversation. Or just walk away without casting judgment.

When you have nothing useful to say, keep a "noble silence." Bring the practice of listening into this practice of talking. Let silence be an integral part of the whole experience. As soon as idle chatter falls away you will be more attentive to your talk-partner and to yourself. Talking will become more meaningful. No words will be wasted. No unnecessary chatter will clutter the atmosphere and serenity will prevail.

EATING

Another truly delightful mindfulness practice. In the Zen Buddhist tradition, meals are ritualized and taken in silence. Chants that invite mindfulness and gratitude are recited, and no one begins eating until everyone is served. Only as much as can be eaten is taken. No one goes hungry. No one overeats. During the meal everyone pays attention to just eating. At the conclusion of the meal, there is more chanting as everyone is reminded of his or her purpose for the day and in life.

This beautiful practice can be easily adapted to our hectic Western lives. Here's how:

- **Plan your meals.**
  You know the needs of your body better than anyone

does. Whether you need frequent, small meals throughout the day or do best with the usual three, it is important to schedule them.

- **Confine your eating to mealtimes.**

  If your body needs nourishment in the afternoon between formal meals, plan that into your meal schedule; even if it's not a full meal consider it as important as the others.

- **Do not eat on the run.**

  It is dangerous both nutritionally and otherwise to eat while driving or walking or doing anything else. But be flexible. There are times when we need to break the rules.

- **Make a ritual of it.**

  Set the table, light a candle, say a prayer. Whatever fits your personality. Create your own meaningful eating practice. Include your family and friends.

- **Turn off the TV and just eat.**

  It's okay to have a conversation while eating; in fact, it's a great time for families to come together and share their plans or their experiences during the day. But let there be no other distractions. Be together (or alone) and just eat. Serve yourself only what you're sure you'll eat. Be mindful not to waste food. Bring a sense of gratitude to the simple fact that you have enough (probably more than enough) to eat.

If you are the one who cooks, take this same mindful approach to the preparation of the food. When chopping, just chop, when stirring, just stir. The meal will then be infused with your mindful energy, which will then be transmitted to those who eat what you have lovingly prepared.

So, when eating, just eat. And in so doing, be like Buddha.

PLAYING

You might wonder why there's a section here on play. This probably seems like one area of your life where you don't need help. This is where you know how to be present, mindful, happy, and serene. This is where, whether it be during a tennis or Monopoly game, while running or bowling, you've experienced losing yourself and just playing. Even if you don't take the time out very often anymore, even if you have to summon childhood memories, you do know how to play and enjoy it. You don't need to be taught a thing.

There are only two things to say here. One, play as often as you can. And two, take what you know in this realm of your life and apply it elsewhere.

While at play, we can be both serious (we want to play our best and win) and lighthearted (it's about having fun and not the end of the world if we lose), and we can get so completely absorbed that we become "one" with whatever it is we're playing. But if playing has become so serious a pursuit for you that there are times when it's not fun, then it's time to look at that and begin to change it.

Go back to a time in your life when you weren't so serious, when playing was what it's supposed to be. Bring that child-mind into your present-day play-activities. Then when play is once again fun, bring this mindset into other areas of your life. Carry a sense of play to work with you, into your relationships, and out into the community. Whenever you begin a new and challenging project, approach it in a balanced, playful way, with a serious yet lighthearted attitude. This may take some practice and you'll never be "perfect." But isn't that what play is all about? Focus on loving the doing of it as you love the playing of play. Put the consequences out of your mind and just be in the moment-to-moment engagement.

As you develop your habits of mindfulness, your self-awareness will increase. So whenever you become aware that you are in a much more solemn mood than the occasion calls for, or you are taking things much too personally, take a moment to regroup your faculties and encourage your mind to enter into a play mode. In other words, lighten up.

Play always utilizes the body. Go for a fast walk or a run around the block to help you shift gears. Notice that when your mind is serious and self-involved, your body is most likely tense or highly agitated. When you move your body, you will stir your mind. And then laughter, or at least a deep smile, will be possible. Anytime you get close to this, you are that much closer to serenity. So call a friend who makes you laugh or read something funny and transform your too-serious mood into a more playful one. Just by way of a smile, your whole attitude and outlook will change.

TASKING

If you're a typical, modern human being with too much to do and not enough time to do it all, you probably spend a considerable amount of time just thinking about what you have to do before you actually do it. Let's first look at the thinking half of this process. You already know how obsessive thinking can disrupt your peace of mind by projecting you into a future that hasn't yet arrived. Anxiety builds up as you worry about all that you have to do and when you might do it. Because it's impossible to do all those things at once, and because you cannot accomplish anything just by thinking about it, you begin to feel overwhelmed before you even begin.

As soon as you recognize that your mind has moved forward in time, bring yourself gently back to the present by taking a few deep breaths and noticing where you are. What color is the wall or sky in front of you? Who are you with? What are they wearing? Even if you are surrounded by strangers, observe their different forms of dress. Then refocus on whatever it is you were doing and know that the chores ahead of you will get done when you get to them. If your mind continues to project ahead into thinking about all you have to do, and you can't concentrate on the present moment, take out your notebook and write a daily task list, a weekly task list, a monthly task list, and a sometime-in-the-future task list. If you have time, prioritize each list. Then put the notebook away and return to what you were doing.

Now let's look at the doing side of this process. When

you get to the doing of the first chore on your list later that day, or the next, bring your full attention to it. If it's the laundry, concentrate completely on separating the colors from the whites, on loading the machine, on setting the dial, on hanging up or folding each article of clothing. Bring to this chore a feeling of gratitude for the fact that you have clothes to wash and a machine to wash them in. Be grateful for the running water and electricity that make this chore possible and quite simple. Involve yourself one hundred percent in this activity. If you notice that you are thinking ahead to the completion of the task, pull yourself gently back to whatever your hands are doing in this moment and imagine what you would be feeling if you were doing it for the very first time. Open your heart to the miracle of your hands and feet and legs and whatever else you are utilizing to accomplish this chore; and be grateful for your ability to complete this task.

Whether it be washing the dishes, sweeping the floor, raking the yard, or building a tree house, bring your complete and focused attention to the doing of it. Each time your mind wanders, gently coax it back. When you are engaged in doing a chore that has been particularly distasteful to you historically, use the opportunity to learn more about yourself. Bring yourself back to the first time you did this chore or to the time when it turned sour for you. Forgive whomever or whatever it was that you believe responsible for your present attitude (even, or most especially, if it's you) and remove all the emotional baggage from the current-day task at hand. And then do it as if for the first time and shift your negative attitude into a positive one.

Since it's not always easy to go directly to a positive outlook, use the practice of mindfulness to take you there—be utterly and completely in the present moment, in the doing of the task at hand. When cleaning, just clean; when cooking, just cook; when raking, just rake. This practice will encourage positive thinking and prepare you for the ultimate task of just being. Do the chore to do the chore, nothing more. And in the doing of it, just be.

DRIVING

Like riding a bicycle, once we learn how to drive a car our body remembers and we no longer have to think about it. On automatic pilot, we start the car, shift into gear, step on the gas, and off we go. Of course we check the mirror, look over our shoulder and watch for oncoming traffic, but all of this is done as reflex action. Once we are on the road with the cruise control on, our mind searches for something to do. So we pick up the phone or eat our lunch or listen to the radio. But what if you took this time to just sit and just drive, in silence?

Pay attention to your body in the seat, your outstretched arms, hands on the wheel. Check your breathing. Consciously slow it down and deepen it, silently saying "deep" on the inhalation and "slow" on the exhalation. Be attentive to the traffic flow, the hum of your car, the wind in your hair—being still and being in motion simultaneously. Serenity in motion. Many of us easily slip into the mindless version of this—which can be very dangerous—and all it takes to turn it into mindful driving is to employ some of the tools you've learned so far.

Even if you haven't expressed road rage or leaned heavily on the horn in an attempt to move traffic forward, chances are you have experienced some frustration behind the wheel of your car. While driving mindfully and serenely on an open road is available and appealing, most of our time is usually spent in the more stop-and-go local traffic situations that are ripe for sowing irritation. Usually, we are in a hurry to get someplace, and the red lights always seem to be against us. We often end up behind a student or a seemingly inexperienced driver. We want an explanation for the traffic jam. Our patience gets tried. We lose our temper. Our mind becomes engaged in the futile task of willing circumstances to change. Any serenity we had going in gets completely shot. Whew! We're out of breath just thinking about it.

Given that you cannot change the traffic, the first thing you can do is let go of your desire to do that. Accept the situation as it is presented to you. Take advantage of this time to generate mindfulness. Be completely present to your body sitting in your car on Main Street. Notice the time, the slant of the sun, the other drivers' faces. Be aware of your need to change how it is at this moment. Relax into being frustrated, being slowed down, and finally into being you. Acknowledge that the other drivers around you are probably feeling some frustration as well. Send them some positive energy. Smile at them. Share the experience of being there. Laugh at your collective predicament. And then when you finally get to your destination (and remember you can't get there until you get there) you will be relaxed and ready for the next thing, in harmony with everything as it happens.

The city version of the above might take place sitting on the edge of the bus or cab seat willing the traffic to move faster or the driver to drive the way you would if only you were driving. First thing to remember is that you're not in control of how the traffic flows or the driver drives. Then it's just a small step to sitting back and enjoying the ride.

BATHING

There are certain daily practices that we all engage in to maintain our physical and mental health, with eating, sleeping, and bathing being the three main ones. Whether you're mindful of it or not, most likely you already have established habits of bathing. It is probably a daily act that takes place at about the same time, at least five days a week. You may have a set routine in how you wash your body— top to bottom, or vice versa. Chances are that you have habituated this activity to the point where you don't have to think about it. Which allows you to wander off in your mind and look ahead at what might be waiting for you the rest of the day.

Most of us also take for granted the fact that we have hot running water, and rarely consider that water itself is becoming a scarce commodity. While every activity is an opportunity to practice mindfulness, bathing is especially perfect because we can usually arrange to be alone, there is little to distract us but our own mind, and it feels good. Begin to transform your bathing experience from mindless to mindful by establishing a ritual. Do it in silence. Bring all your attention into the bathroom. Establish a new pattern of washing your body and be attentive to each detail. Draw your mind to each body part as you wash it. Without luxuriating in the feel of the water, be mindful of its pure quality and direct your mind into an attitude of gratitude. (Luxuriating in a hot tub of scented water surrounded by candles and soft music is a different experience and one to be taken every so often, if you are so inclined. It can be a mindfully relaxing time and quite different from your daily bathing routine.)

Each time you bathe is an opportunity to practice mindfulness and establish gratitude—a good start to your day. It can also be one of the times each day when you remind yourself of the third leg of the tripod of contentedness: spiritual health. Along with physical and mental health, your spiritual condition determines how grounded and content you will be in your body and in your life. Too often, this third leg gets neglected so that our serenity becomes wobbly and unstable. Rather than seek a spiritual solution, we often resort to shoring up the other two legs by eating or sleeping more, which further destabilizes our condition. Just as healthy eating practices determine our physical health and sound sleep contributes to our mental health, let your bathing practice be one of the ways you confirm your commitment to spiritual health. As part of your ritual, before stepping into the tub or shower, make a vow to yourself to be completely present as you bathe. Then just wash your body as you begin practicing mindfulness. When finished, seal the experience with another vow to continue this mindfulness practice throughout the day.

And remember that every suggestion in this book is merely a suggestion. If you are committed to living a mindful, serene life you will take what works for you, discard the rest, and create your own unique ways of keeping your tripod of serenity healthy.

WORKING

It's unfortunate that the routine of working has such a bad rap these days. Since we spend the bulk of our day working, our attitude toward it determines our level of harmony in relation to it. So if we are stuck in negativity—blaming our boss, the job itself, and the long hours we spend at work for our distress—no matter how our work evolves we will stay stuck until we shift our attitude. The bad news here is that it's entirely up to you—not your boss, your situation, or the money you make—to change.

The good news is that it's entirely up to you. You and only you have the power to transform the effect work has on you. Only you can transform a feeling of dread when going to work into joyful anticipation. Sometimes you may discover that nothing short of leaving your job and moving on to something else is the answer. But most of the time all you need to do is adopt a positive attitude. This may not happen all at once and it may not happen naturally. So the way to get to a positive attitude is one step at a time, one task at a time.

Bring your full attention—your entire body, mind, and spirit—into the *doing* of each work activity. If your task is dependent on someone else and they're not cooperating, move on to the next thing, rather than get caught in the web of griping and waiting and, hence, not working. When you notice yourself thinking about coming to the end of what you're doing or about how nice it will be to finish work for the day, bring yourself back to the project at hand and be unconditionally in the *doing* of it. If your to-do list or in-box or some unfinished business or unpleasant task is gnawing at you to be done, take the time to do it, mindfully, respectfully, and diligently. Leave the negative attitude out of it. Just make the phone call, write the letter, or file those papers—whatever it is. And it will be done. It will no longer take up space in your mind. Thus, you will start to create new work habits, begin to feel better about each job and about yourself as a worker. Positive thinking will begin to replace negative thinking and your attitude will naturally lean toward the positive without having to take any giant leap. You will exult in the *doing* of whatever it is you must do whenever it is that you must do it. Work will no longer be a bad word and something outside of you—it will become intrinsic to who you are. Your life will be a seamless flow of positive energy with work an integral part. All you have to do right now is turn the page and the rest will follow.

3

The Practice of Being Challenged

Just getting through a typical day without ending up exhausted or embittered can sometimes be so daunting that when faced with some of the larger challenges of life we seem to have no energy resources left for the fight. So we let the major events take control and toss us to and fro, all the while thinking that we have no choice. But we do have a choice. We *can* face all the challenges that life serves us, big and small, maintaining our serenity in the process. We can even learn to roll with the punches so that nothing takes us by surprise and we stay on course even when the turbulent winds blow.

At this point you've established a foundation built on concentration and mindfulness. Together with these you can now engage some energy to see you through the challenging times and situations that are bound to arise. When you set time aside—even if it's only ten minutes a day—to be still and concentrate on your breath, your energy reserves will continually be replenished and you'll be able to summon up some energy whenever it's needed. This will allow you to work with determination through each challenge as it appears. It is important to keep in mind here that when you are committed to this practice you will never be given more than you can handle in any given day. Trust that. You have the resources. You have the power. You have the energy to face all challenges and come to the other side—whole, serene, and content with the knowledge that you stepped up to the plate and gave it your all.

Once you begin the practice of being challenged, you will even come to view challenges as opportunities rather than obstacles. You will be empowered by them and shrink from nothing. And you will grow in ways that might surprise you. But because you will be well versed in these practices, you will accept it all as naturally as you embrace the inevitability of the rising and setting sun. You will see that your life is like the weather—changeable, unpredictable, sometimes cloudy, sometimes sunny, but always perfect and just as it should be.

EGO

The idea, or rather the reality, of an ego is paradoxical. On the one hand it gives us a healthy supply of self-esteem, which in turn provides us with the necessary energy to face the world and its inherent storms. On the other hand it can drive us so deep into self-consciousness that all we can see is ourselves, which leads to a very closed and negative existence. Let's call the first ego our worthy-ego, and the second our petty-ego.

When our worthy-ego is engaged we cling to nothing, we carry no hate, no fear, no jealousy; we concern ourselves with others and are able to see the larger world and our place in it. When petty-ego is active our world gets very small; we only care about the world around us insofar as it will give us what we want; we define and relate to everything in the first-person singular, the "I," the "self." This is a very treacherous zone. And until we establish a strong and consistent practice of concentration and mindfulness it is usually our petty-ego that has the loudest voice and the strongest control over us. Our practice here is to distinguish between the two egos and whenever petty-ego rises up notice it and then drop it.

Petty-ego is our conditioned mind, and if we remember

that everything changes, that nothing is permanent, then we can conclude that ego too has no consistent nature, that it is not a fixed phenomenon. This makes it easier to discard when it appears. There is a Zen saying that will help here:

"The occurrence of an evil thought is a malady, not to continue it is the remedy."

Replace "evil thought" with "petty-ego" and you're on your way to creating yourself anew each moment, to not relying on conditioned ego, and to being present in *this* moment.

True freedom is attained when we gain freedom from the tyranny of our ego, from our desires. When we are in our petty-ego we see ourselves as the center of the universe. When we drop our petty-ego we can see that we are not the center of the universe, but a part of it, and that each part is interconnected and integral to the whole. This automatically leads to unselfish behavior that benefits you and the universe. And this lifts your worthy-ego, diminishes your petty-ego, and results in a grateful and serene mind.

RELATIONSHIPS

There is probably nothing that challenges us more than our relationships, since every aspect, every nuance of our life involves a relationship of some sort. Every waking and sleeping moment we are engaged in a relationship with something or someone—with our spouse, boss, children, friends; with co-workers, store clerks, strangers; with our thoughts, dreams, body; and finally with ourselves, our Higher Self and our God, whatever that means to you. So in many ways this area of practice is the ultimate one, the final frontier, the one that we can acknowledge without a second thought is ever-changing and never-ending. We are never completely alone, for even when any given relationship is not active there is still a connection with that person. And it is important to remember that our behavior affects those we are in relationship with and vice versa. Paradoxically, however, we are alone and solely responsible for our actions.

Here's how the practice of being challenged in relationships works:

- Whenever the behavior of someone else bothers you, turn your focus around, observe your reaction to this person, and ask yourself what it is about this that disturbs you so much, and why.

- Know that you cannot control anyone else—you can be a guide and a teacher and a power of example, but you can never determine how someone else will ultimately think or behave.
- Practice giving others the freedom to express and be themselves as they uniquely are, without expecting them to conform to your idea of who they are or who you'd like them to be.
- Communicate; communicate; communicate.
- Listen; listen; listen.
- Let the most important human relationship you have be the one with yourself; from there you will be able to love others.
- Don't take anything too personally.
- Don't take anyone or anything for granted.
- Look to your pets to learn about unconditional love.
- Express yourself. And rather than pointing out to someone that their behavior is bad or wrong, let them know how their behavior affects you. Keep it all on your side of the street.
- Be alert, aware, mindful, caring, generous, forgiving,

loving, gracious, and kind to yourself and others. All the time. Every moment.

And when there is trouble and discord in a relationship you might take the following advice from St. Francis:

"...grant that I may seek rather to comfort than be comforted—to understand, than to be understood—to love, than to be loved."

Say this or some other favorite prayer each day. And trust that as the above prayer also expresses, "It is by forgiving that one is forgiven."

FAILURE

Failure is merely a matter of opinion, time, and attitude.

Opinion: failure is bad.

Whenever something happens—especially if it doesn't conform to what society and we think is the optimal scenario—we judge it as bad and look for someone to blame. The one who usually gets the brunt of it in the end is the one who has "failed." For instance, if you were to get fired from your job, even if economic conditions and the state of your company were responsible, chances are that at some point you and others would blame you, especially if some people kept their jobs.

Time: we never know how time will transform events.

What is thought of as bad can often turn out to be good after some time passes. Example: after being fired from your job you go on to pursue the career of your dreams, which would not have happened without the job loss.

Attitude: keep it positive because you never know.

Rather than falling into negative thinking—"I'm no good, I'll never work again, how will this look on my résumé"—engage in positive thinking by seeing the "failure" as an opportunity. For example, "Now I can take that class, start my own business, or change my career focus." When one door closes, another one opens.

When confronted by an event you would normally define as failure, the practice is: don't be so quick to judge it as bad; let time be the judge; and keep a positive attitude.

Decide that the universe is doing you a favor and helping you create something that you couldn't do on your own. Consider it a gift and it will be. Another opportunity to practice gratitude.

SUCCESS

The *Tao te Ching* says: "Success is as dangerous as failure." This is a succinct way of saying that if we allow either success or failure to carry us away, off the ground and into a realm of illusion, chances are we'll come crashing down at some point and the fall will hurt. This doesn't mean that if you're enjoying success you will eventually fail. It means, if you stay grounded you will maintain your equanimity and be able to accept whatever happens.

Some of the traps that success can set:

- **Complacency.**
  Once we're successful, there is a risk that we will consider our work done and begin to take success for granted. Boredom can be one result; followed by laziness, followed by the disappearance of success.
- **Judgment of others who are either more or less successful.**
  To support our insecurities we might view those less fortunate as inferior and those more fortunate as lucky.
- **The "never-enough" syndrome.**
  No matter how much success we gain we remain dissat-

isfied, always wanting more, never grateful for all that we do have.

- **Self-aggrandizement.**
  We boast, we strut, we gloat, forgetting that success can be taken away as quickly as it was given.

> A caution: Watch out for that green-eyed monster of envy and jealousy. When others succeed, be happy for them; congratulate them if you know them, send good wishes if you don't. There is plenty to go around, and spending your energy on envy and jealousy only depletes you and detracts from your own success. Rather than envy others, emulate them. And stick with the winners; spend time with them, learn from them, love them.

Your practices during successful times:

- **Continue working with determination.**
  Allow your goals to be malleable and ever-changing; avoid the trap of thinking that you've made it and reached the end. Life is a dynamic, ever-evolving phenomenon, and so it is with accomplishments. Stay committed to your path.

- **Practice charity toward others—in your thoughts and deeds.**

  When you taste success, be willing to share it. Wish the same for others and help them where you can. Such generosity benefits everyone, and as the saying goes: "In order to keep it you have to give it away."

- **Call on your worthy-ego, not your petty-ego, to gain perspective.**

  You deserve success; you worked hard for it. So don't let your petty-ego drag you into stingy thoughts and behaviors. Resort instead to your worthy-ego or Higher Self. Be grateful.

Remember that life is a process and every day brings new challenges, rewards, joys, and sorrows. With every experience we learn new things. Nothing is stagnant. This is why we call it life. So sit, breathe, and move through your life with energy and determination. If you do, you will know success.

FRUSTRATION

Indeed, we all have suffered frustration, and sometimes we let it carry us into a state of anxiety and depression. From experience, we know that that state of mind never relieves the frustration, it only aggravates it. Let's take a moment and look at the common source of frustration and then how we might avert it.

Generally, frustration seeps in and takes hold of us when our needs go unfulfilled and our problems remain unresolved. It begins with a desire for something and a craving for resolution. This wanting is only human. It is our attachment to the outcome that causes us so much discomfort.

When you feel the slightest twinge of frustration, take a few moments to determine its source. Look again at what it is that you want, and see if you can notice the real difference between that and what it is you've been given. Maybe it's simply the same thing packaged differently. Maybe it's something altogether different and something you never could have imagined. Be open to letting this new thing in and letting go of your original wanting. Maybe it's better. Maybe it's just different.

The practice here is not to give up your wanting—you are, after all, only human—but to be aware of it and where it takes you. Practice going after what you want and preparing yourself for the manifestation of it, however it comes to you. Be open to all the possibilities. Let go of the ending you've already written for your life. Be present to the way in which your life unfolds without attempting to adjust it to your vision of how it ought to be. What your life has in store for you is even greater than you can imagine, so give yourself over to it. Do the work, then let go and delight in the wondrous nature of it. Learn to live life on life's terms and frustration will be kept at bay.

DISAPPOINTMENT

Expect nothing. It cannot be stressed too strongly or expressed too often. Expect nothing. If you can simply contemplate these two words and practice them day and night there's no need to say or do more. Expect nothing.

Something as simple and innocuous as waiting for a promised phone call can lead to disappointment. The caller gets legitimately delayed, you heard the time incorrectly, or there's some other reason the call comes later than expected or not at all, yet you still experience disappointment. When disappointment lingers even after you learn the facts, it may create resentment if you cannot forgive the assumed source of your disappointment. Disappointment can lead to frustration, blaming, anger, and our own bad behavior; so unless we can learn from our disappointment and not react to it, it is best for all concerned to avoid it whenever possible, and, as already stated, the way to this is to expect nothing.

If you're sitting by the phone waiting for the call that doesn't come, your experience might look something like this: you go over in your mind exactly what was said regarding the phone call and determine that you're right, the call is late. You blame the delinquent caller. You get frustrated, worried, angry, and then hugely disappointed. Your expectation is dashed and frustration sets in because you didn't get what you wanted when you wanted it. (Especially if you weren't engaged in the practice of being still and just waiting.)

If you tend to sink into disappointment when something doesn't happen as you imagined it would, were told that it would, or expected it would, then the only antidote is to eliminate expectation. Accept that anything can and will happen, that sometimes the actual outcome will turn out to be even better than anything you could have foreseen, and that you might miss this other, new, and unique scenario if you are sitting with blinders on, stuck in your tunnel-vision viewpoint.

Know that the stance of expecting nothing takes time to cultivate and much practice to perfect. And also know that it doesn't mean just giving up and becoming a doormat. It simply means that flexibility as opposed to rigidity is called for. You have innate resources to assist you—your breath, your belly-mind, your heart, your intuition, even your intellect. Call on them all as you face the challenge of being disappointed, and eventually disappointment will be but a tiny blip on your screen of serenity. Changing circumstances will not blow you off your course; you will welcome the unpredictable nature of all things; and you will handle the challenges of your life as smoothly and as gracefully as you sleep. Peace will come if you persevere.

AMBITION

When we practice bringing ourselves into the present moment throughout the day, it can sometimes be very confusing to know how to handle our dreams for the future, our ambitious career and personal plans. If we let our minds take us into this territory, it can get quite tumultuous indeed. We might ask ourselves such questions as:

If I'm always in the moment, how can I plan my future?

If I don't spend time looking ahead to my future, how will I ever achieve anything?

Isn't it important to look at my past mistakes, the opportunities I missed, my failed plans, so as to avoid similar pitfalls now and in the future?

The only thing these questions will do is take you out of the present and disrupt your peace of mind. The only thing here you need to know is: if you don't enjoy the process of moving toward something, you'll never enjoy being there, if and when you arrive.

So here are a few tips to help you enjoy your journey:

- Work toward something; but if you're not enjoying your day-to-day activities, rethink your decision.
- Avoid tunnel vision. Don't be so focused on your goal that you miss other opportunities along the way that you would enjoy pursuing.
- Loosen your grip. Allow the dream to change as you change.
- Be flexible. Don't think that there is only one path to achievement.

- Don't decide to stay on your chosen path no matter what—be open to new and different paths.
- Be available to a scenario that you didn't write the script for.
- Always consult your belly-mind when facing a decision.

Ask yourself the following question, which is more about life than about death:

If you knew that you had a short time left to live—six months, a year, two years—how would you spend your days? What would you change, if anything?

Remember, your life, your future is happening right now. **This is it!** All you have to do is be present for it. Take a deep breath, fill your whole body with air, and exhale through your fingers and toes. And now settle into your life.

Breathe in and out once more. Repeat. As many times as necessary.

Not only are you right here, right now, but you are also already there.

OPPORTUNITY

Opportunity doesn't always present itself to us as we might expect. It comes in many shapes, sizes, and forms. It can appear when we least expect it and seem absent when we most expect it. It is fickle and unpredictable and yet always available if we're open to it. But due to our habitual patterns, biases, and ways of seeing, we don't always hear it even when it comes knocking loudly on our door. Our internal music is way too loud. It sometimes appears in the periphery of our vision but blinders keep it from our view. And our expectations cloud everything.

So, first, turn down the volume, take off the blinders, and put aside your expectations. Easier said than done? Doesn't have to be. That's a choice. It is a challenge, though, and one that you have to be willing to face. That's all it takes: willingness. The rest is easy. It all flows from that. Endless energy wrapped in determination courses through you when you turn on the tap of willingness.

And then let opportunity court you. Your job is simply to be available and open. Take risks. Some will bring rewards as predicted, some won't. It's the natural ebb and flow of things. The risks you take that don't produce the results you wanted or expected often lead to other choices. Watch out for them. Be alert, be mindful, be positive.

Remember to keep your balance. Stay centered, focused, and flexible. You have the tools; all you need do is employ them. If you've already forgotten (it's easy to do, so don't berate yourself), keep in mind that it's all about practice, practice, practice—progress not perfection.

Usually we define opportunity as something that, if taken, will benefit us personally. This is basically true, but it's not always as direct as we might think. So, let's look at some of the myriad opportunities that are presented to us every day, ones that carry multiple gifts. Like the opportunity to:

Serve others
Practice charity
Say nothing
Just listen
Practice proper behavior
Keep noble silence
Be tolerant
Forgive
Pay attention
Trust

Learn
Be generous

And how about these situations that create opportunities for growth:

An argument with a loved one
Not getting what you want
Losing something you have
Getting what you want
The behavior of others
The unexpected

These lists are endless. Add your own ideas of opportunity to them. Be creative. Allow the world in and practice with your heart wide open.

COMPETING AND COMPARING

It's hard not to do it. The world today seems to be all about it. It starts when we're small children and never lets up. The message we get from society is to vanquish all opponents and win no matter what. So competing is just a matter of course, part of the game, an integral part of life. What we may not realize, though, is that it sets us up to compare our skills, talents, and resources with others. This practice seeps into every aspect of our lives so that we end up constantly looking out at what others do, say, and have; always comparing and left wanting. Rather than winning anything, we end up losing ourselves and all hope for serenity.

Just as too much thinking causes disquietude and a disturbed state of mind, so too does comparing and competing. And just as you cannot simply stop your thoughts, you also cannot stop comparing and competing just because you think it's a good idea. With your busy mind and racing thoughts you learned to invite stillness in by switching your focus to your breathing. With this practice of continually drawing your attention to your breath, deepening your breath, and stilling your body, your mind activity slows down, the silent gaps between thoughts get wider, and serenity begins to settle in. You can use this experience to help you develop a technique that will reduce your comparing and competing tendencies and lead to a higher level of self-esteem, an honorable life, and respect from your fellows; all of which will contribute to your serenity.

The first key to this practice is awareness: before you can

change anything you must become aware of where you are and what you do. So pay attention. Each time you feel resentment toward someone for what they have, feel "less than" in someone's company, or realize that your focus is completely other-directed, turn your focus around. Without judging yourself for what you're feeling, simply recognize your tendency to compare and compete, notice how it erodes your serenity, and draw your attention back to you. Acknowledge yourself for who you are and what you've done, without placing anyone else alongside you. (It is important, though, to recognize and honor those who have helped you and have contributed to your life.) Keep turning your focus back onto you. You are no one else and most likely when you consider the matter deeply you truly do not want to be anyone else. Draw a sense of gratitude into this self-image. You have your own unique life path, and others have theirs. The longer you spend on your own path and avoid those diversions into others' territory, the stronger you will be, the higher you will hold your head, and the more others will respect you. So, as we touched on before, applaud the success of others but remain with your two feet firmly planted in your own life. This is where it all will happen for you. Stay put, be grateful, and you will eventually lose the need to compare and compete.

LOVE

We are social creatures and the relationships we cultivate throughout our lives give meaning to it. Whether or not we express our feelings of love every day to those we love, we know without question who these people are. We could make a list in a minute that would contain our loved ones. Take some time to do that now. The order is not important. Just write a list of all those people you love today. Include those you once loved who are no longer active in your life. This may take more than a minute, but don't think too hard about it. Write from your heart.

If someone comes to mind and you find yourself hesitating to write their name, start a second list of questionable loved ones. Perhaps you're holding on to some anger and don't feel loving at the moment, or you're not quite sure if your feelings toward them constitute love. If they pop into your mind put them on one of these lists. And if your love of someone has turned to hate, put him or her on the list as once-loved.

Scan down the first list, the unequivocally loved, and note when you last expressed your love to each. Make it a point the next time you see them to let them know how much you care. Or if you won't see them anytime soon, communicate your feelings from afar. There are many ways to express love, so be creative. Saying the words "I love you" may be the easy way out. Go out of your way without being extravagant—send a beautiful postcard or their favorite jar of jelly. With those you live with or see every day, make your expressions of love a daily habit without expecting anything in return—give your partner a foot massage; spend an afternoon with your niece. Love simply for the sake of loving.

Now for that second list. This presents a real opportunity to open your heart and love unconditionally. Chances are whoever is on this list has disappointed you or hurt you in some way, has not given you what you need, or has not returned your love in kind. This will be hard, but put aside for now whatever they did or didn't do to you. Decide that whatever it is you want from them will never be forthcoming. Then ask yourself if you still love them. If the answer is yes, then let go of your need to change them or to have them do something that doesn't come easily to them—and just love. Do something nice for them without expecting anything in return. Do something loving without letting them know who did it. And bask in the joy of love.

If the answer is no, then wait a day or two and ask again. If the answer continues to be no, ask yourself if you ever loved them. If they're on the list, chances are this answer is yes, and all that relationship needs is an adjustment. But nothing will change and your serenity will continue to be compromised until the hate disappears. So embrace this feeling of hate. Draw in hate; release love. Then reverse it. Draw in love; release hate. Let the love you feel for all those on your love list overwhelm the hate. As you already know, if hate gets a hold on your heart there's little room for love and all your love relationships get infected. So, embrace the hate, then let it go; and let those sour relationships take their course with only love in your heart.

4

The Practice of Being Present

When we're disturbed about something, dissatisfied with our life, or simply feeling the blahs, chances are we're thinking about the past or projecting into the future. Too often we live for tomorrow: the anticipated raise, the hoped-for romantic partner or excursion, the time when the kids will be out of the house and on their own. We stare into the future at our plans, hopes, and dreams, confident that the magic elixir, the panacea for our troubled mind and heart, will be there waiting. We continue to live in the delusion that someday our prince will come (or whatever our version of the fairy tale is) and when he does all will be well, forever and ever, till the end of time.

You don't have to be told that something is wrong with

this picture. You might, however, need to be reminded of the alternative; the alternative you sensed is there. You've tasted it—it is always available to you and within easy reach. If you submerge yourself in it, everything makes sense and joy abounds. What is this magical solution? Just this: Now. The present. This moment. It doesn't mean that life won't continue to be unfair at times, and unpredictable most always, but it does mean that if you live in the now you will know how wonderful life is, even with all its ups and downs.

Joy is only possible when you are in the now. It is not present in the past or in the future. Recall some of your most joyous times and you'll know the truth of this. You have the chance to live in joy every day, with everyday people, doing everyday things. You needn't wait for the prince. It's not that he's not coming. It's that he's already here.

If you were expecting something grand, something outside yourself, something to sweep you away and carry you into a permanent state of bliss, the news here will be disappointing. But if you can, for just one second, entertain the idea that the truth is even more spectacular than that, then you will know joy, contentment, and serenity in this lifetime.

BROKEN SHOELACES

How many times has a broken shoelace spoiled your morning or whole day? If your first answer is never, because you have no shoes with laces or you've never broken one, keep in mind that broken shoelaces is simply a metaphor for all those little things that happen unexpectedly— always at the wrong time and in the wrong place. Things that by themselves cause no harm and have little significance, but that nonetheless impose themselves on us and often interfere with the smooth running of our lives.

Spilt coffee. A flat tire. An empty container of milk in the refrigerator—again. A toilet seat left up or down. An unkind word. A red light when you're in a hurry.

I'm sure you can come up with your own list. It would be a good idea to do that right now. Write a list of the little things that have happened lately, even today, that have contributed to altering your mood or your behavior. Then, look beyond the surface. Rather than focusing on the broken shoelace and deciding that if only it hadn't broken you'd be just fine, look past that. First look at how it affected you. Did you get angry? Did you express or repress that anger? Did you use it as an excuse to do or not do something? Did you blame someone else or even yourself?

Avoid justifying your reactions and slipping into your habitual pattern of dealing with things. Do not judge yourself. Simply take notice of the ramifications of the broken shoelace in as detached a way as possible.

Then look deeper, with no judgment, and see if you can discover why broken shoelaces have the effect on you that they do. Maybe, just maybe, your reaction to the broken shoelace has nothing at all to do with the broken shoelace. If so, take note of the real source. There's no need to do anything. Just pay attention, observe, and acknowledge what it is. Let the truth reveal itself. And then do nothing. Just admit it and sit with it. Breathe it in. Breathe into it. Then move on. And the next time you're faced with a broken shoelace, take a deep breath and remember this little experiment. If you don't catch yourself right away, repeat the above and again look beyond the surface. Do this each time you are faced with a broken shoelace. Before you know it you will glide right through those once irritating moments. You may still feel the pinch, but you will no longer get tossed around by the unexpected breaking of a shoelace. You will deal with the inconvenience, replace the shoelace, and move on.

If there is nothing beneath the surface of the broken shoelaces, but they keep breaking and disturbing your peace of mind, you have two options: buy a different brand of shoelaces, or wear shoes without laces.

CHOCOLATE

It is so easy to take the small things in life for granted. Even when we move up to the bigger things, we take them for granted as well. We have much to be grateful for—from hot and cold running water, to toothpaste, to computers and phones. You know this, of course, and you probably also know that you suffer the human tendency to always want more. What you may not realize is that this craving contributes to your discontentment and lack of serenity, and that it will not abate on its own. You must confront it, recognize its hold over you, and then let it go.

Let's say chocolate is one of your favorite treats. You look forward to your midafternoon chocolate break, you reward yourself regularly, and you sometimes overindulge in it. Sometimes it assuages your craving, but many times it does not, so you eat more than you'd like and end up feeling worse. Yet time after time you think that it will relieve something, so it becomes a vicious cycle. (If chocolate is not what ignites this insatiable craving, surely there is something else, perhaps money or power? Only you know what it is for you.)

You might think that completely giving up your favorite thing is the answer. Not so, although there are situations where abstinence is the best solution. Usually all you need to do is pay attention and not expect chocolate to be more than chocolate.

The next time you eat chocolate be completely present to eating the chocolate. Pay attention to its shape, color, texture, smell, and finally, taste. Take your time. Breathe deeply as you eat. Notice any impulse to eat quickly or more than you'd like. When your mind moves away from eating the chocolate (and you mindlessly put more in your mouth than planned), gently draw your mind back to eating chocolate. Introduce a feeling of gratitude into the activity. When you are grateful for chocolate, then gratitude for all other things in your life will follow. After eating your chocolate, write a gratitude list. Head the list with chocolate (or whatever else you are focused on and grateful for at that moment), and remember to include your breath on the list, for without that nothing is possible.

Every time you become aware that you are taking something or someone for granted, take some time out and write down those things you are grateful for. Doing this daily, even without the chocolate, will help you to avoid taking anything for granted. So pay attention to the small things in life and everything will fall into place.

THE WEATHER

What is it about the weather that can so powerfully impact our moods? We know we have no control over it, yet we often take bad weather—i.e., weather that doesn't fit into our plans—personally. We groan and gripe and sulk when it rains on our parade. We let it ruin our day. I doubt there is anyone who hasn't at some point been negatively affected by climatic conditions. We sometimes have difficulty letting rain or cold or heat just roll off our backs. Perhaps the influence is subtle and we don't even associate a gloomy mood with the weather outdoors. Or perhaps it's the indoor atmosphere that unduly disturbs us. We allow the mood and behavior of others to determine our own level of anxiety or serenity.

No matter if it's nature or human behavior, the first thing we must acknowledge is that the atmosphere outside of us is not in our control. We can no more govern how others think and act than we can affect the rotation of the planet. But we do have the power to manage our reaction to the weather. Once we recognize this we can see that it isn't the weather that determines our mood, it is our reaction to the weather. *If it's cold, shiver, if it's hot, sweat.* If it rains when you want sun, change your plans and express gratitude for the rain, which sustains us all. If a drought comes, do your part to conserve water and appreciate that all individual efforts contribute to the whole.

As far as the weather is concerned each day, you must let it do its thing as you do yours. And if you are fully present in each moment and mindfully aware of your actions and reactions, the weather will take care of you as you take care of it.

CHANGE

In New England, people are fond of saying: "If you don't like the weather, wait five minutes." While this is an exaggeration, the fact is that the weather is unpredictable and changeable. Since this quality of impermanence also applies to everything else, we can adapt this saying to our everyday lives: "If you don't like _____, wait five minutes." Fill in the blank.

"If you don't like:

how you're feeling
what someone is saying
someone's behavior
the crowded streets
the clothes in your closet
the person you live with,

wait five minutes."

You might have to wait a little longer than five minutes, but of one thing you can be sure: in time, something will change. Hence all the notions regarding time, such as: time heals all, time waits for no one, and it's only a matter of time. On the other hand, if you sit around unhappy with the way things are, waiting for them to change, you could wind up hugely disappointed. As an ancient Chinese proverb says:

"If we do not change our direction, we are likely to end up where we are headed."

This tells us that if we want things to change it's up to us. We cannot usually change the external environment (people's behavior or a crowded street, for example), but we *can* change our attitude. Adopting a positive attitude leads to positive changes. And remember, before you can change, you must become willing to change.

So why then, if we know that change is inevitable, do we long so desperately for certainty? Why do we try to lock things into place? Why do we project into the future, and when our lives don't conform to this mental picture, are we surprised? Perhaps because we want, need, and think we have control. But from our own experience, we all know that we really don't. So your everyday practice here is to accept what is and engage the practice of letting go when you can't. This happens more easily when you admit that the only thing you can be certain of is change—and the only change you can control is change from within.

Then decide what it is that you can change, what it is that you can't, and say the following prayer each time your grip tightens around the controls:

> *God grant me the serenity*
> *To accept the things I cannot change,*
> *Courage to change the things I can,*
> *And wisdom to know the difference.*

MONEY

Nary a day goes by when we don't make, spend, think, debate, or argue about money. It can be the focus of our obsession, compulsion, greed, anger, or delusion. We may even think it can save or destroy us. We feel good when we have money in our pockets, and bad when we don't. In short, we give it a lot of power. Even saying that money is a necessary evil imbues it with a quality that it doesn't inherently have.

It is not a bad thing to want money, to have money, to spend money. According to Buddha, two of the four things that contribute to our happiness in this world involve money: we should (1) protect our money and (2) live within our means. (The other two factors are: [3] having good friends and [4] skill in our profession.) Buddha also said that there are four kinds of happiness, of which three are related to money: economic security, freedom from debt, and spending money generously on family and charitably on those in need. But the fourth and most important kind of happiness is spiritual in nature. That is, we should live a good life and not commit evil acts, think evil thoughts, or speak evil words. So even Buddha acknowledged that money is necessary for a happy existence, but if the pursuit of it is our sole purpose, happiness will evade us. We cannot make money our God.

Every day you have an opportunity to experience happiness as you make, spend, and save money. But if you notice that you're placing undue emphasis on it and its rewards, then it's time to pay attention to your spiritual condition. Know that money is a critical ingredient in your happiness quotient, but if your life is not grounded in spiritual practices then all the money in the world won't matter.

There's really no mystery to what constitutes spiritual practice. Intuitively you already know what this means. And the more time you spend quietly with yourself listening to your inner voice, the more you will trust your intuition. And then with this pure mind you will enjoy all the gifts that your money affords.

SEX

First, let's assume that the sex we're talking of here is sex with an appropriate, adult partner with whom you have a conscious and loving relationship. In this context, sex is a beautiful and intimate expression of the bond between you and your partner. It is an opening to discover yourself and another in the physical realm. It is also an opportunity to practice trust and letting go; to communicate love in a special way; to be completely in the present moment; and to connect with your partner beyond words.

Contrary to what many people believe, living a spiritually mindful life and sexual satisfaction are not mutually exclusive. In fact, when we are present in every moment throughout the day we can continue to carry it into the sexual act, which will enhance the whole experience. Approaching sexual relations with an open, honest heart and mindful concentration can be immensely pleasurable.

Just as with other daily activities, bring a sense of ritual and reverence to the act of making love. Have it be a part of your day without the burden of being special. Leave your brain and your ego outside the door of the bedroom and let the experience of sex be one of heart and body.

If you and your partner are having sexual difficulties, chances are it's not the only area of your relationship that needs attention. Most likely it is a communication problem. Do not expect sex to solve other issues or for your partner to read your mind. Sex is a way to communicate beyond words, but sometimes the words have to come first. Talk to each other. Take the time to clear up misunderstandings that won't be put aside just by shedding your clothes. If you carry resentments into the bedroom they will get communicated in one way or another, and will interfere with pleasurable lovemaking. Clear things up as much as possible before sex so that sex can be unencumbered. If you would like something from your partner sexually, bring it up before you are engaged in the act. Communicate what it is you'd like and then let go of all expectations.

Practicing the art of letting go throughout the day in all your activities makes it that much easier to do it during sex, where it is especially important. When we sit with ourselves in silence and delve into our belly-mind, we can say that we metaphorically strip ourselves naked. We let go of the hold our ego has on us and stare into our true nature. In the bedroom, with our love partner, we continue this practice and add the literal act of stripping naked, which places us in a very vulnerable position indeed. When sitting alone and practicing being still, as thoughts come, we let them come; and rather than holding on or following these thoughts, we just let them go. In the bedroom we extend this practice to inhibition, fear, and self-consciousness. We notice, we suspend judgment, and we let go of whatever interferes with our being present. With this letting go we make room for trust. Trust in our partner, in ourselves, in love. Trust that there's a shared commitment present and a caring for each other that transcends our petty, selfish desires. When we can let go, trust, and be present like this, two become one. There is no separation; there is true intimacy. Sex becomes a unique experience and one that can inform the rest of our lives. It can give us a taste of what true freedom can mean when we embrace the interconnectedness of all beings.

Love, and allow yourself to be loved. Relax, enjoy, breathe deeply; be creative, caring, and unselfish. Simply let go and be present to the joy of sexual union.

5

The Practice of Letting Go

Whether we plan the major events in our life, such as marriage or graduation, or simply take them when they come, like birth and death, they often cause stress and discomfort, even when the occasion is desired and celebrated. So how do we keep our wits, maintain our serenity, and sail through these times with grace? Simply by relaxing into them. We practice this by keeping our bodies and minds flexible; and we get to this state through the practice of concentration, mindfulness, energy, and joy.

One huge impediment to our serenity when we face the "big stuff in life" is the uncomfortable feeling of not knowing. The only balm for this is letting go. Letting go is easiest when we're in a relaxed state of body and mind.

By all means do your homework, find out all you can about the circumstances you find yourself in and take whatever actions are necessary. Be educated. But at some point you must come to the realization that you can't know the end of the story—how long and happy your marriage will be, when your parents will die, if your career will turn out as dreamed. And at these points you must let go if you haven't already. Holding on only creates more tension, pain, and suffering. And this produces even more extreme circumstances, which creates even more tension, which leads to other conditions, and so forth. The only way to break this progression is to relax and let go of trying to control the outcome. There may be nothing you can do or change about the state of affairs, but you can come to an understanding about it and your reactions to it, which will lead to a more relaxed state, which will help you in the process of letting go. This too is a progression, but a positive one, which leads toward the realization of serenity even in the midst of chaos.

This may all seem fanciful and impossible to achieve. Not so. Yes, it takes practice. And yes, you may not always be perfect. But if you decide that you are willing to change your usual, habitual patterns of processing the major events in your life (or for that matter, every event in each day), then it will be possible for you to relax, let go, and experience serenity. Practice with the smaller things in life first, so that by the time the big things come around you will be ready. This new behavior will become so second nature that you won't even have to think about it—a good thing since there's little time for that when you're facing the big decisions.

Let the future take care of itself by settling into not knowing, and relaxing your body and mind. Keep a positive attitude, be mindful of your words and deeds, and embrace your feelings. See things as they are and then let go.

DEATH

It is inevitable that, no matter what our economic or social status is, one day our physical body will die. This is irrefutable. There are a lot of theories about what happens to us—our spirit, our soul, our karma—after we die physically, but no one really knows. And we also do not know when our time will come. Living with this not knowing can cause a great deal of anxiety and fear. Sometimes, without even being conscious of it, we become so afraid of dying that we hold on to life tightly enough to squeeze the life out of it. Afraid of dying, we become afraid of living. In this state it is almost impossible to overcome our fear of dying. Rather than attack it from that end, let's instead look toward the life end of this spectrum. Let's accept for now that we are only human and that death scares us. Then notice that right now you are alive. Put the thought of death aside for the moment and trust that today is about life. Celebrate that. Embrace your life. Be grateful for it. And take one small action today that expresses this.

How well do you take care of your body? Do you eat well and mindfully? Do you get enough sleep? Do you exercise regularly? If not, you have some work to do. In your quest for serenity, it is vital that you take proper care of your body. Do not think that a spiritual life of serenity occurs only in the mind. Your body is an integral part of this process. The healthier and more flexible your body, the healthier and more flexible your mind. And vice versa. There is a symbiotic connection, and this relationship feeds your spirit, which resides in your belly-mind, which sits in your abdomen, which is part of your body. If you take good care of your body and mind, you automatically take good care of your spirit.

One important way to take care of your mind (and by extension, your body) is to carry a positive attitude. Not only does this keep your mind flexible and in synch with your life, but recent clinical studies show that being positive will actually extend your life by as much as seven years.

When your body and mind are relaxed, your desperate hold on life relaxes, and you begin to enjoy life's moments more than ever. Like a strong, deeply rooted tree you are able to bend without breaking even in the strongest gale.

As the ancient spiritual philosopher Lao Tzu says:

> *The hard and inflexible*
> *are disciples of death.*
> *Thus, the soft and yielding*
> *are disciples of life.*
>
> *There are no winners among the rigid.*
> *If a tree won't bend it will snap in two.*

So, live flexibly, centered in your spirit. Take care of your body and mind. Live fully and richly. And you won't be afraid of the unknowable.

ILLNESS

From minor aches and pains to more serious health issues to life-challenging diseases, no one is immune from normal human suffering. But these occasions need not drain your life spirit, nor rule every aspect of your life. They can even grant you an opportunity to step aside from your usual existence, take an honest appraisal of things, and reestablish priorities.

The body can often be wiser than the mind. And when we nurture the habit of consulting our belly-mind, we learn the truth of this. But before we become adept in this practice our body might get our attention by shutting down, which will force us to stop and take a break. This does not mean that all illness is a wake-up call—sometimes a cold is just a cold—but how many times have you fallen ill simply because you needed a break and were unable to take it? How many people do you know, perhaps yourself included, whose lives have been transformed by a grave illness? Whether it's a major or minor setback, sometimes we don't attend to our spiritual well-being until the body breaks down. Here are a few suggestions:

- Take good care of your body; avoid gluttony and the abuse of intoxicants.

- When illness strikes, take the necessary steps to treat the symptoms, and then pay attention to whatever message there might be in it for you.
- When ill, be ill. Avoid labeling it as good or bad.
- Be positive. The state of your mental health will affect your physical health.
- Be honest. If falling ill is a means you use to escape the demands of your life, begin looking at other options and what you can do to alter this course. Be brave to be healthy.
- Get the medical help you need, but don't rely completely on anyone else; participate in your own recovery.
- When others become ill, know that you cannot save them. They have their own process. All you can do is offer your loving support.
- Remember the body/mind connection. Eat well, exercise often, and get plenty of sleep.

When you take care of yourself—your body, mind, and spirit—you'll be surprised at how healthy you become, how infrequently serious illness strikes, and how prepared you are when it does. When you take life in stride, even illness won't toss you off the path.

LOSS

Whether we like it or not, loss is a fact of life. What we often don't remember, though, when we're suffering the pain of losing something or someone, is that there is always something gained to set the scales back to balance. We may not notice the gain right away, and it may not appear immediately, but if we keep our eyes and hearts open to this truth then we need not plunge into the depths of despair when loss visits.

Each year the trees lose their leaves. Each year they return. Even if we have a personal preference for a particular season, we know that no season is absolutely superior to another. They are simply different, with their own unique qualities. Yet even with a phenomenon as unpredictable and changeable as the weather, we can experience sadness when our favorite season ends or when the climate on any particular day doesn't suit us. This is simply the very human tendency to want what we want when we want it. The only remedy for this is to keep a positive attitude, accept whatever comes to us, and know that sooner or later everything changes.

At this juncture, it is imperative to see that while we do have control, at the same time we have none. On our journey into serenity perhaps this truth is the most difficult to embrace, but it's the most important. The real is not rational and can only be expressed paradoxically. Loss can only happen after we've gained something. And so the reverse is also true. Nothing lost, nothing gained.

While loss may not feel so terrific, keep in mind that it only feels bad because you had something that you thought would last forever, and it's the holding on that causes the pain. So let go, experience the loss, and relax into the natural ebb and flow of life. Sometimes, after some time has passed, the loss itself can be seen as a gain.

There is a common ritual of childhood, which helps prepare us to deal with loss—one that we can resurrect and continue to use as adults. Remember the tooth fairy? It helped us as children to learn that a lost tooth wasn't a tragedy and that in good time there would be another. Loss followed by gain. The gift under the pillow simply served as a token to assuage the pain of loss and as a reminder that nothing lasts forever and new growth will occur. We are never too old to be reminded of this lesson. So when something treasured disappears, be your own "loss fairy," and do something to remind yourself that loss is not the end of the story and can be transformed into a gift.

Life may be unfair and it may be unpredictable, but it is

also wonderful. And in this wonder loss becomes one of our greatest teachers. When we respect this, gratitude soars and we reap the benefits of loss as surely as they are there.

BIRTH

The birth of a baby. The birth of a new idea. The birth of a pet project. All joyous occasions, full of possibility. So why then do they sometimes hurt so much? Because the true nature of life is paradoxical. Because we're human we forget and hold on to the idea that good things feel good and last forever. No matter how many times we learn otherwise.

First, understand that every human life contains some difficulties, which in turn cause discomfort, dissatisfaction, and/or outright pain and suffering.

Second, recognize that most of our real discomfort or suffering comes from our desires—for things to be other, different, better than they are—and our attachments to outcomes.

Third, realize that we can eliminate our suffering by seeing things as they are and letting go of our craving and clinging.

Fourth, follow the path to spiritual wholeness, integrity, and ultimate freedom.

Think of this process as a new birth, a new you. Give up your old ways of handling life, and adopt a new approach. Let go of entrenched ideas, and be open to new ways of seeing. Reach down into your spiritual center, your belly-mind, each time you are confused. The right answer will reveal itself in time. You will know what to do and say when you put your petty-ego and pride aside and let your heart and spirit decide. Take time each day to nurture this new outlook. Be mindfully aware of your thoughts, actions, and speech. Take care not to judge yourself or others too harshly. Be patient, yet determined.

Imagine yourself walking slowly through a thick fog. When starting out you are completely dry. As you move through the foggy mist you begin to feel damp. Gradually you get wetter and wetter until you are dripping with a wet-ness that you cannot even see. So it is as you move through the process of spiritual rebirth. You may not even notice the changes right away. But if you keep on the path you will eventually become so saturated in this new way of being that you hardly have a memory of your old ways. Just keep walking.

CELEBRATIONS

The unstable trinity of Western holidays: Thanksgiving, Christmas, and New Year's. There's so much to celebrate; yet November to January is the most stressful time of year for many people, contributing to states of depression and anxiety, from mild to debilitating. And then there are all those other occasions we create to celebrate our accomplishments and ourselves: graduations, engagements, birthdays, and weddings, which too often turn out to be more trouble than they're worth. Why do these events, which are meant to buoy and entertain us, compromise our serenity, induce depression, or strain relationships with loved ones? In a word: expectations.

It's one thing to joyfully anticipate a special event, it's quite another to look forward with expectations of how everything will unroll and play out. This is dangerous territory. It always and inevitably leads to disappointment. Not one of us has a crystal ball. No one can predict how things will turn out. Whenever we have a vision of the future in mind, it always turns out to be different. If we're looking for it to be the way we imagined and hoped for, even if it turns out better we can be disappointed. We may notice the improvement, but we rarely appreciate it.

The solution is to expect nothing. At first, this may seem not only impossible but also inhuman. If so, take a second look. Practice by living fully in each moment as it comes and in the small daily events. When you notice yourself projecting into the future—even if it's only minutes or hours or days ahead—consciously and mindfully draw your attention back to the moment you are actually in. Use your breath to do it, use your body to do it, use your mind to do it. Completely and gently guide your expectations into your breath and toward your belly-mind. Fill your belly with your vision of the future as you inhale, and release your hold on it as you exhale. Continue this exercise until there is room in your breath, belly, and mind for whatever will be. Practice this frequently, especially during times of celebration. If you practice this during calm times you will automatically resort to the practice during times that test your composure. And when the occasion to celebrate is upon you, you will be there for it, in a mood to celebrate.

Then begin to develop this habit: every time you suffer a disappointment, take some time to trace it back to its origin. Chances are you'll discover it was born of an expectation. The natural progression of this is to eliminate expectations and then reduce disappointment. Then celebrate all the truly wonderful moments of life without any unnecessary baggage. You are the architect of your own life. Celebrate and practice that by being mindfully present in each and every moment, letting go of all expectations.

VACATIONS

Do the planning and preparations for your vacations ever cause more stress than the intended relaxation is able to cure? Do you ever find that you derive more satisfaction from your vacation in the aftermath—telling stories and looking at photos—than in the actual experience of it? Do you so look forward to vacation time that days and weeks go by where you're more in the upcoming vacation than you are in your present day-to-day life, and then when the actual vacation arrives it is less than you imagined and wanted it to be? Do you live for your vacations and get most of your enjoyment of life from taking time away from your normal routine?

There is nothing wrong with taking a vacation. In fact it is a very healthy thing to do. But when it interferes with, rather than contributes to, your serenity, you need to ask: what is wrong with this picture? Consider honestly the following statements and which, if any, apply to you.

- I regard vacations as a panacea for my troubles.
- I use vacations to run away from upsetting circumstances in my life, hoping that they'll disappear or be forgotten upon my return.
- I expect vacations to relax and soothe me so that I can return to my life renewed and refreshed.
- I am more truly myself while on vacation than at any other time.
- Vacations afford me the time and space to decide how and with whom I want to spend my life.

Any of these puts an awful burden on the vacation. No wonder it sometimes falls short. Here are some simple suggestions that can help take the pressure off and reinvigorate your vacations with pleasure.

- View your vacation as an extension of, rather than as separate from, your usual life.
- Be wary of any and all expectations attached to vacations.
- Approach vacations as you've learned to do with the rest of your time—mindfully and moment by moment.
- Be open to plans changing at the last minute and to the unexpected. Let yourself get lost.

- The main theme of most vacations is relaxation, one form of letting go. If you practice this way of being in your day-to-day life you'll be prepared when your vacation rolls around. When you return you'll be renewed and refreshed.

JOB LOSS

"I heard the news. Congratulations. Terrific! Wonderful! What a stroke of luck."

If you lost your job and someone said these things to you would you think they were:

(a) uncaring and insensitive, or
(b) wise and perceptive?

The normal, conventional choice would be (a), and if you lost your job (b) would seem not only preposterous but also cruel. Yet (b) is the better choice, and here's why: we never know how events will unfold, and we limit ourselves when we view the world in dualistic terms; i.e., losing job is bad; keeping job is good.

Invariably, when one is "relieved" of one's job, the knee-jerk reaction is fear. There may be lots of other emotions mixed in as well—such as anger, shame, or relief—but fear colors them all. Even if we dislike our job and often wish it away, if it is taken from us, we tend to keep holding on. We want to know what's next; we grasp after security and certainty. We panic when we lose what we thought was secure and worry about how we'll feed our family and pay our bills. Some of the practical matters, like temporary loss of or reduction in income, are serious, but there is always a solution, which we can't see if we're in a state of panic. The simplest solution to the immediate financial crisis (which most of us focus on as the BIG problem) is to ask for help to get through the short term. Help is always available in some form, though pride often blurs our vision and erects such a huge barrier that we often don't even realize it's right there in front of us.

Is there security and certainty inherent in any job? No, not really. Can the loss of our job ever be a good thing? Yes, nearly always. If we cling to our job and delude ourselves by thinking that the security and certainty (however false) are worth whatever displeasure our job creates, we limit our choices. In this state of fear, if we are relieved of our job, we are not prepared for the subsequent emotional turmoil. It can then be difficult to take advantage of the opportunity that losing a job offers us. Losing a job (regardless of the reason) can grant us some free time to spend assessing what it is we want to do next in our lives. It can be a gift that we wouldn't have given to ourselves that allows us to pursue a long-buried dream. It can be the kick in the butt we needed to make a change that deep in our heart we knew was inevitable. It can be the wake-up call we were waiting for that will help us transform our work life into a meaningful affair. It can signal the end of a life half-lived and the beginning of a life fully realized.

Think of being fired as something that the universe is doing for you that you couldn't do for yourself. Resist the impulse to blame and recriminate. Breathe in your fear and breathe out courage. Trust that even if you loved what you were doing there is something more magnificent awaiting you. Continue to iterate that this is a precious opportunity, not to be wasted—the chance in a lifetime that not everyone is given. Each time negativity appears, take it in and turn it upside down. Flip that coin on its tail. You've been given some time, so take it; don't rush toward the answer. Time takes time, and when it's time you will know what to do and how to proceed toward the only possible, positive next step for you. Be brave, even as you feel afraid. This is when the journey can get positively exhilarating and you can become fully engaged in the moment-to-moment movement of your life. Don't allow a little thing like fear to rob you of this growth opportunity. Carpe diem!

6

The Practice of Being Aware

It is in the arena of feelings that most of us get tossed around unwittingly. Sometimes feelings (especially those we label negative) can be so powerful that we let them rule our lives. We tend to resist and push away the feelings we don't want and hold on tightly to those that we wish would last forever. Even though experience teaches us that neither approach is effective for maintaining serenity, we continue to behave in this way because it seems to make sense to us. We push away that which we don't like and hold on to that which we do. In this section, you will learn about practices that seem counterintuitive, i.e., embracing the feelings that you want to be rid of and letting go of those you want to keep.

What we are aiming for is balance. Equanimity. Evenness of mood. What our habitual thinking tells us to seek is happiness ever after, endless joy, eternal bliss—especially if we read fairy tales as a child. We believe in these childhood promises even though we know that everything changes, that nothing is permanent. It's not that joy isn't available to us—it most definitely is. But if we want to live in a state of serenity we must view the world realistically, and accept that a full life contains all feelings, good and bad. Our job is to live in the paradox of reality and know that we are more than our feelings, that whatever our feelings in any given moment, they'll eventually pass, and that we have the power to transform our feelings.

For every feeling there is an opposite feeling. Would we even know joy without suffering? Hope without despair? Anger without compassion? Surely most of us would rather there be only one side to the feelings coin (the "good" side); but obviously this isn't possible. So, for now, as you work with the practice of feelings, put aside your dualistic measure of things and refrain for the time being from judging anything as good or bad, right or wrong. Be open to a new way of looking at things. Turn your usual point of view upside down and inside out. Let go of the need to know before you know. Then you'll be ready to explore and live in a state of well-balanced self-assurance, where no feeling will seduce, overwhelm, or control you. Composure under all conditions will prevail and serenity will be yours.

PAIN

This may be the one overriding feeling that we'd all like to avoid, be it of the physical, mental, emotional, psychological, or spiritual variety. But there is no life without pain. Even in birth, the most spectacular and miraculous event in life, there is pain. Yet even when we accept that pain is a part of life and unavoidable, we still go to extreme lengths to not feel it. Here is an exercise that you can do daily that will help you understand your relationship to pain and teach you to manage all sorts of pain. If you persevere, you will discover that pain can be your friend.

Begin by sitting completely still for ten minutes a day, and build up to forty minutes once you establish a practice. Erect your spine. Begin in as comfortable a position as possible, with no overlapping, interlaced arms, legs, or fingers. Concentrate on your breath. Keep your eyes open. Don't move. No matter what, don't move. If you get an itch, don't scratch it. If your leg falls asleep let it be. If you think of something that you must do right away, stay seated and continue breathing. The itch will fade, your leg will eventually wake up (and there will be no permanent damage, no matter what your mind tells you), and the chore that needs doing will be waiting for you.

As you sit, notice your resistance (which is, by the way, normal). Watch how this resistance can intensify the pain. Practice breathing into whatever pain comes up and just letting go. Use your breath to manage your physical pain. Observe yourself—your reactions, thoughts, feelings, impulses, and projections vis-à-vis your pain. And do nothing. Just keep sitting through it. Whenever you become aware of being in pain, change the thought of "I'm in pain," to "pain." Take the "I" out of it. See the pain simply as pain, nothing more.

Here are some things you might experience and learn about physical pain if you practice this exercise daily:

- All pain passes (or at least changes).
- The thought of future pain can intensify current pain.
- Resistance to pain accentuates it.
- It is never as bad as we think it is.
- Accepting it and breathing into it lessens the impact and often releases it.

- Wanting it to be something other than what it is makes it worse.
- We create some pain merely for the entertainment value.
- Over time, with practice, it gets physically easier to sit still for the allotted time.
- We become better able to handle painful situations when not doing sitting-still practice.

If you practice sitting with pain, then whenever pain arises, on whatever level, you will intuitively know what to do with it. Each time pain pays a visit in any area of your life, you will reach for the techniques you honed while sitting still to help you. You will see how pain is often just an illusion that disappears in due time as long as you don't hold on to it. You will also realize that pain is a normal part of human existence and that suffering with it is optional.

Pain is one of our greatest teachers. Make friends with it, let it instruct and guide you toward greater clarity and purpose.

NEGATIVITY

There may be nothing that interferes with serenity more than a negative attitude. Not only that, a negative attitude can be detrimental to your physical, mental, and emotional health. It's a vicious cycle. The only thing that can interrupt this cycle is to adopt a positive attitude. No matter what.

The popular epigram of Murphy's Law, "If something can go wrong, it will," points to how endemic negativity is. Not to mention easy. But think about this: if it's so easy to predict and create negative situations, why can't it be just as easy to turn that around and replace the negative with the positive? Well, it *is* that easy. All it takes is awareness, a decision, and an action. Which will lead to change in habitual patterns; which will create space for new, positive habits to develop.

No matter what the external landscape in any given moment happens to be, remember that you have the power to choose your mental environment. The first thing to do is to become aware of your negative thinking. If you are displeased in any way, chances are you're thinking in a negative fashion. Don't judge, just notice. Then decide that you want to reverse this manner of thinking and that changing it is up to you. Own the negativity. Breathe it in. And then breathe out positivity. Keep doing this until you notice a shift. You may have to practice it throughout the day if you're having a particularly difficult day or if a negative outlook is deeply ingrained and habituated. Don't give up. If you continue this practice and keep the clear intention that a positive attitude is truly what you want, then you will replace negativeness with positiveness.

Keep in mind the law of cause and effect. Negative thoughts and actions create negative results. Positive creates positive. But watch out for those expectations. Being positive doesn't mean that everything will go your way and that you will get everything exactly as you want it. Simply be positive and let go. Holding on is about fear, which is the mother of all negative attitudes. So use your greatest gift, your breath, to help you establish trust in letting go. Breathe in positivity. Breathe out negativity. While it may seem counterintuitive, it also works the other way. Breathe in negativity. Breathe out positivity. Try it, and just keep breathing.

HOPE

Have you ever made any of the following comments? What do they have in common with each other? How do they get you in trouble?

- Let's hope that never happens again.
- Let's hope for the best.
- If only I could _____ I would _____.
- Imagine how nice it would be if _____.
- There's always hope.

> Instead of saying: I wish this war would end and peace would come.
> Ask: What can I do to achieve harmony in my life today?
>
> Instead of thinking: I hope he finds his way.
> Ask: What can I learn from his experience?
>
> Instead of: I hope I get that job.
> Ask: What can I do today? What am I doing today?

Hope is something that we all call upon when the going gets rough. While I'm not the first to say it and it may sound blasphemous, try this instead: Give up all hope.

What does hope accomplish other than take us out of the moment, project us into an unforeseeable future, and build up our expectations? What is hope but a desire for change, a wish for circumstances to be other than what they are?

It's not wrong to hope to get better, for instance; it's just not a good idea to live solely in that hope. Bring yourself into this moment and be completely present. Deal with whatever is right in front of you now. Pay attention to the sound of your breathing. Admire the abundant colors all around you. Be grateful for your life as it presents itself to you.

When we give up all hope we can't help but be right here, right now. And only when we are in the present do we have the opportunity for peace of mind, serenity, and true contentment. Being present allows us to appreciate the gifts in our life and marvel at the way life moves.

Life is unfair. Life is unpredictable. And though you may think you'd be happier if you could call all the shots and make things happen to suit you, if you sit still long enough and listen to your deep truth, you will know how false this is. What choice do you have but to accept the unpredictability of life, go with the flow, and see how wonderful your life already is?

So, whenever you notice yourself hoping for something different, breathe into your belly and out through your toes. Feel the air enter your nostrils and follow it as it fills your lungs and expands your rib cage, diaphragm, and belly. As you slowly release the air, feel your body relax into itself. Breathe in peace. Breathe out hope.

You can also try this another way. As you inhale, breathe in all the hope that you and others you know are feeling. Think of all those in dire circumstances and breathe in the hope that they must be holding on to. Then breathe out peace. Think of all those people receiving this peace that you are exhaling into the universe.

Try it both ways whenever you reflexively begin to hope. Train this new muscle that you are developing and breathe away hope. It might take some time, but before too long your outlook will shift and be more consistently positive. There's no need to hope. Simple as that.

JEALOUSY

It's so easy to look at the behavior of others to justify our feelings. But no matter what other people do or say, we are ultimately responsible for our own feelings. You could probably convince anyone who will listen that another person's behavior is deplorable and it's natural for you to feel the way you do. But isn't that giving them all the power over how you feel? How does giving away your power affect you? Can you do something to reverse that? Without my saying so, of course you know that you can. Intuitively you know that only you are responsible for how you feel.

Jealousy is a tricky one. Often, it is precipitated by a loved one acting inappropriately and not considering your feelings, or by an imagined indiscretion, or by comparing, or wanting, or coveting. More often than not, we create scenarios in our mind to feed this green-eyed monster. Usually it has little to do with the truth, the real circumstances. Mostly it has to do with the fear of losing something or someone we have, or not getting something or someone we want—our petty-ego engaged. And our self-esteem is often at issue whether we realize it or not. Because we're so intent on watching and imagining the antics of others, we cannot even see ourselves in the picture.

So the first thing to do when jealousy rears its ugly head is to do an about-face and look in the mirror at yourself. Investigate the source of the feeling. Divorce it from the current target. See how far back it goes. Then admit that at the core of the jealous feeling is love. Focus on that. See how fear gets into the mix to disguise and obscure the truth. Keep focusing on the love. Express those love feelings to the person who has aroused the jealousy. Take a risk. Express yourself, your truth, your love.

Don't expect anything back. Luxuriate in the pure nature of giving. Withhold nothing. Spend it all. When you do this, love will come back to you tenfold. It may not come from where you're looking, so be prepared and open and available for anything. Don't lock yourself into any corners you can't move out of. Open your heart wide, and love, not jealousy, will be your reward.

MOODS

Some people wake up naturally each morning in a sunny disposition immediately ready to greet the day. Others struggle with moodiness first thing and need time to sort themselves out before facing whatever awaits them. There are morning doves and there are night owls. Which are you? We might get it in our heads that one temperament is preferable to another, that one is better, superior, the one to aspire to. This is again just our black-and-white outlook operating, which requires us to define some things as good and their opposites as bad. This dualistic point of view does us a huge disservice. The first thing to do here is to suspend judgment, so that we can see clearly without the cloud of guilt that usually hangs over the moods we've categorized as bad.

Even when we adopt a positive attitude toward life there will still be times when we'll feel sad or lonely or discontented or just plain dull—moods that we've been programmed to define as bad. But if we can remove that label and just allow ourselves the emotion, whatever it is, we can then get in touch with a valuable piece of ourselves that needs expression. And when we do this we're less likely to wallow. If we repress "bad" feelings, they sometimes force themselves on us; since we're unused to feeling them, we may not even know how to describe them when they do surface. It's important to allow all feelings; because repressed feelings only end up causing dysfunction and ill health in the end. Let the feelings come, identify them, let them run their course, and let them move on.

You may find that as you awaken to the whole range of feelings, those you once considered bad may redefine themselves as good, and vice versa. For instance, expressing sadness about a lost relationship might bring you closer to a current one. Articulating your feelings enables you to put them behind you and live more fully in the gifts of the present. Regret disappears and love blossoms.

When we are in close touch with how we're feeling at any given moment, and when we embrace whatever feeling is there, we have the best chance for maintaining our equanimity. No one feeling gains prominence, we spend less time on the extremities of the feelings-spectrum, and we reside smack in the center of who we are—without shame, guilt, apology, or superiority. It's about balance, about being human, and about reserving judgment.

FEAR

More than anything else, fear can interfere with our having a serene and fulfilling life. It can keep us from doing those things that we most want to do and being with those we most cherish. It can rule our life if we let it. Even when we become aware of its power, we still gravitate toward it and quite simply choose to let it have reign over us. Fear can be a familiar and comfortable place. It seduces us because it is predictable and grants us the illusion of control. It also helps us keep the mystery of things, people, and places alive. We believe that if there's no fear, there's no mystery.

By confronting your fears you can overcome them. It's likely that you're not even in touch with what scares you, so identifying your fears is the first step in the process. Begin by making a list of everything you feel afraid of, from simple everyday matters, to the larger, more complex life issues. Your list might include some of the following:

Roller-coaster rides
Airplanes
Social gatherings
Failure
Success
Ridicule
Intimacy
Being wrong
Rejection
The unknown
Allowing your dreams

At the core of all fear is the fear of disappearing, of annihilation, of not being accepted, understood, or loved. This all adds up to the fear of dying. It is only human to have this fear. The problem is it too often keeps us from truly living. We must stop running from ourselves, stay put, and give expression to our fears. Naming begins the process of rendering our fears powerless. It gives us enough courage to investigate the fear, sit with it, and do the opposite of what it would have us do.

You are not your fears. You are also not responsible for having the fear. All you need concern yourself with is your reaction to fear. When you face fear and decide to not let it control you, the subsequent actions result in greater self-esteem, a sense of accomplishment, renewed vitality, and freedom. Fear then begins to recede. It loses its grip on you when you don't let it take hold.

Fear may never disappear completely—after all, we are only human—and it can take on a subtlety that can surprise us. But in time, when we take on our fears, our joy of living grows exponentially, death becomes just another life event, and the mystery of life continues.

JOY

Such a small word for such a big feeling. How often have you used this word to describe your mood? Are you one of those people who hold it in reserve for special occasions, for the grand moments of life? There is so much pressure to have everything perfect before we employ this word to describe how we're feeling that we hardly ever use it.

If you want to experience more joy in your life, begin to notice how you verbally express your feelings. Are you more skilled at describing negative, painful feelings than positive, joyous ones? Whether this is true for you or not, start to pay attention to the small details throughout this day that impart a feeling of happiness, no matter how minute they might be. Your morning cup of coffee; an Op-Ed column by your favorite writer; a fresh, juicy orange in the middle of the afternoon. Mark these experiences as joy moments. Take the time to savor the feeling—without expectation, projection, or comparison. Let it be what it is, in the moment that it is.

Sometimes we take for granted the small joy moments that occur each day and let the more disturbing feelings, which may also reside in each day, color our overall mood. This can lead us to believe that we are generally discontented, causing us to wish and hope and dream for a more joyful existence. We think of joy as something to attain, to aspire toward, something that someday will be ours, permanently. But there's no need to wait. There are joy moments in every day for each of us. We simply have to notice them, name them, and be in them. By doing this we will bring a sense of balance to the day, and then, by extension, to our whole life.

In everyone's day, in each of our lives, there are good times, there are bad times; there are joyous moments and sad moments. If we participate in our life, take things and feelings as they come to us, without unfairly judging or getting swept away by any of them, we can create a life of equanimity. Thus, joy will be a part of every day. We will no longer have to wait for the BIG feeling of JOY. It is there for us to have any moment, anywhere. No big deal. And yet a very big deal indeed.

ANGER

Plays have been staged around it. Volumes have been written about it. Wars have been waged because of it. Relationships have disintegrated, health has been compromised, and serenity has been lost altogether. All in the service of anger. And what is it but a reaction to the way things are and a desire to have them otherwise? More often than not, anger is triggered in our relationships with others. We rail at their behavior and treatment of us because we know a better way, the right way, to behave. Often it has nothing to do with us. Mostly our anger derives from our self-centered fear. When things don't go as we want them to, or think they should, we become afraid of disappearing. Our defense is anger, followed by some attempt to manipulate circumstances to our point of view. Experience tells us that this doesn't work, but we continue to react with anger out of habit.

There is another way. That way is acceptance, compassion, and love. Of yourself and others. This is where your self-centeredness can work for you. Decide that you are as important, not any more or less, than those around you. Don't repress your anger, but before you expose it to others, take a good look at it. You may find that your anger is justified. Even so, ask yourself if it will serve any useful purpose. The answer is always no if you're honest with yourself, and if you don't let your petty-ego and pride interfere. So rail silently, express your anger in writing and perhaps to a confidante. Then let it go. For if you let it hang around, the only one it will destroy is you.

Practice acceptance. This does not mean to be passive. Take action against situations that exist to exploit others, for instance. Use your anger in a positive way. Do what you can and then let go. Use your breath to help you stay in the moment. If you are present to the immediate moment there will be no anger, because the past, future, and even the present will disappear. Then love will have a chance—the only cure for anger.

Each time you become angry, stop and take a look at it. Usually we just let it take charge without even noticing it. So paying attention is the first step toward conquering it. Sit silently with it and observe your anger, without judgment. Rather than saying, "I'm angry," just notice that there is anger. Watch how anger arises and how it disappears. In fact, you can do this with all your emotions, and by so doing, become the detached observer of your own mind.

When you know your mind, you will know yourself. No matter the circumstances, it is up to you to choose your own mental and emotional environment—hopefully one that doesn't honor anger. This is ultimate freedom and true serenity.

Closing Thoughts

CURIOSITY

When we stop resisting and struggling against the parts of our life that we believe we can't abide, and instead investigate our reactions, attachments, thoughts, and feelings, we have a greater chance of achieving and living in serenity. Whenever you are confronted with something that bothers you, practice not shrinking from it. Engage the curiosity that brought you to pick up this book and others like it, to look inside yourself and see what's there. Anytime you become aware that you are searching outside yourself for answers, turn your focus around and look within. By all means, read spiritual literature, attend lectures, and research what the masters throughout history have had to say about leading a spiritually serene life. Then take what you learn and draw it into your body, into your belly-mind, and filter it all through your intuitive personal truth. See how it fits. Be discerning. Trust yourself.

If you're in crisis, seek outside help, and let trusted

others take care of and help make decisions for you; and when you are comfortably back to normal, begin to renew trust in yourself.

When Buddha was near the end of his life, some of his students asked him to impart to them some final words of wisdom, something that they could hold on to after he was gone. They were still dependent on him, so he gave them the greatest teaching of all. He said: "Be a lamp unto yourself." This is inspiring advice and as appropriate now as it was 2,500 years ago. What he meant by this is to rely on yourself, not on others. Rely on the "truth" of life, the truth that your belly-mind, your intuition, your "gut" imparts to you. Trust in this truth. Investigate this truth. Look toward others and learn what you can from them, but in the end decide for yourself what works best for you. By looking into your heart and belly-mind—while keeping pride and ego at bay—you will find all the answers you seek.

Here is a short list of some things you can sit with, contemplate, and meditate on as you progress on your journey.

- What hindrances do I encounter that rob me of serenity, such as ill will, worry, or doubt?
- Who is the "I" that thinks my thoughts or feels my feelings?

- What is mindfulness exactly?
- How does desire help and hinder me?
- Can love and compassion really conquer all?

Sit with your mind, study it, and know it—without judgment or criticism. Be curious about how it works. Delve into your belly-mind. Practice breathing in and breathing out that which pains you and that which comforts you. Let this practice develop into a daily habit and evolve into a meaningful spiritual practice.

When you take the time to quiet your chattering monkey-mind, sit still for a few moments, and listen to your "true nature," you will undoubtedly know right from wrong, you will know what next action to take and when to do nothing. You will learn how to be at peace in your life, which will lead you to be completely awake for whatever life serves you. Your life will then not simply be about your life. It will be about giving your life to be of service to others. And in this giving you will truly be born, again and again, moment by moment. Thus you will have serenity in motion—inner peace: anytime, anywhere.

About the Author

NANCY O'HARA was drawn to Zen Buddhism in the mid-1980s, after the death of her father, and found solace in the profound stillness of silent meditation. In a Jukei ceremony in 1992 Nancy committed to the precepts of Buddhism and was given the dharma name of *Myochi*, which means "wondrous wisdom." All of her books offer spiritual guidance for everyday life based on her own experiences and the teachings of Zen Buddhism. Nancy conducts meditation classes and workshops, and corporate seminars and retreats on mindfulness at work. She lives in New York City. Visit her at www.nancyohara.com